Fostering International Student Success
in Higher Education

2nd Edition

SHAWNA SHAPIRO

RAICHLE FARRELLY

ZUZANA TOMAŠ

This book has a
companion website. Go to
www.tesol.org/FISS
for additional resources.

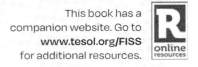

www.tesol.org/bookstore

TESOL International Association
1925 Ballenger Avenue
Alexandria, VA 22314 USA
www.tesol.org

Managing Editor: Tomiko Breland
Copy Editor: Wendy Rubin
Cover, Interior Design, and Layout: AM Graphic Design Ltd

Recommended citation:
Shapiro, S., Farrelly, R., & Tomaš, Z. (2023). *Fostering international student success in higher education* (2nd ed.). TESOL International Association and NAFSA.

ISBN 978-1-953745-06-4
ISBN (ebook) 978-1-953745-07-1

Library of Congress Control Number 2022946612

A copublication of TESOL International Association and NAFSA: Association of International Educators.

Table of Contents

Acknowledgments

We would like to thank our many colleagues from various institutions and disciplines who share our commitment to international student support and empowerment. We would also like to thank the students we have had the honor of working with in our classes and as participants in our research projects. We are tremendously grateful as well to our editor, Tomiko Breland, for her guidance and encouragement throughout the process of revising and updating our book, and to Wendy Rubin for her fabulous copy editing work. We would also like to thank the many colleagues and students who provided feedback on our first edition, informing many of the changes we have made in this second edition. Individuals who were particularly generous in their feedback include Roberto Arruda, Kate Donley, Auli Ek, Iuliia Fakhrutdinova, Aditya Jane, and Cathleen McCarron. We also give a very special thanks to Karen Edwards, the dean of international student affairs and exchange visitors at Grinnell College, who provided us with detailed suggestions throughout the chapters and gave us permission to adapt her visa policies handout for this edition (see Appendix F).

Shawna would like to thank her coauthors, Rai and Zuzana, for developing the original vision for this project and giving her the opportunity to join them as a collaborator. She is also grateful to her former colleagues, students, and research participants at the University of Washington and Middlebury College, who contributed a great deal to her understanding of the needs of international students and best practices for supporting them. She wishes to acknowledge her colleagues in the Center for Teaching, Learning, and Research and the Writing and Rhetoric Program at Middlebury as well, as they have encouraged her to experiment with new ideas for academic support and curricular innovation. Finally, she would like to recognize her parents, Steve and Sheilah Shapiro, whose lifelong dedication to education inspired her to choose this career path, and her husband, Garrett Kimberly, whose love, support, and patience help make this work not just manageable, but truly gratifying.

Rai wishes to acknowledge the personal and professional relationships established throughout her career with language learners, language teachers, colleagues, and mentors at the University of Utah, the American University of Armenia, Saint Michael's College, and the University of Colorado Boulder. These professional and personal relationships serve as the cornerstone for her contribution to this book. She would like to thank Shawna and Zuzana for the pleasure of collaborating on a project that speaks to our shared concerns about equity, inclusion, and justice in education. She is grateful to friends and fur kids who remind her what matters most in life. Finally, she'd like to thank her loving parents, John and Colette Farrelly, who have been instrumental in all of her successes.

Zuzana would like to thank her family—her husband, Aleksandar Tomaš, and her kids, Amelia and Tim. Zuzana is also grateful to her coauthors, Rai and Shawna, and colleagues and community in diverse Washtenaw County in Michigan. Finally, Zuzana would like to acknowledge her parents, Viera and Dušan Šarík, without whose love and selflessness she would have never been able to pursue education and build a life in the United States in the first place.

CHAPTER 1

Introduction

Over the past couple of decades, the number of international students studying in English-dominant countries such as Australia, Canada, the United Kingdom, and the United States has risen dramatically—more than doubling, in the case of the United States (see the sidebar, Growth in U.S. International Student Enrollment, 1996–2020, for more information about enrollment trends[1]). This shift reflects a larger trend of increased study abroad worldwide, including with higher numbers of students from Anglophone countries studying at institutions where other languages are dominant (Canadian Government, 2019; Fuchs et al., 2019; ICEF Monitor, 2019).

In this book, we offer insights and strategies for supporting international students in higher education (i.e., tertiary or postsecondary) classrooms. Our aim is not only to facilitate these students' success in meeting their educational goals but also to tap into the assets and opportunities that can be gained with an increasingly global student body. Although our focus is primarily on the U.S. context, we expect that many of the insights and strategies presented in this book are relevant to other contexts where international students are a key part of the demographic. We mainly focus on the classroom, though we do touch on some broader institutional issues that can impact students' academic success.

It is important to begin by considering the reasons for this increase in international student recruitment. From an institutional perspective, increasing the numbers of international students has several benefits, including diversification of the student body, higher prestige for the institution, and increased revenues during times of

01

Growth in U.S. International Student Enrollment, 1996–2020

Academic Year	Total students studying abroad in the United States
1996–97	457,984
2001–02	582,996
2006–07	582,984
2011–12	764,495
2016–17	1,078,822
2019–20	1,075,469

Countries With Highest Numbers of Students Studying in the United States, 2020–21

Country	Number of students	Percentage of all international students studying in the United States (%)
China:	317,299	34
India:	167,582	18
South Korea:	39,491	4
Canada:	25,143	3
Saudi Arabia:	21,933	2

Source: Open Doors, 2022

---

[1]Numbers have fluctuated significantly over the past few years, due in large part to the COVID-19 pandemic. For this reason, we are only including numbers through the 2019–20 academic year.

economic uncertainty. Internationalization can also create opportunities for global and cross-cultural exchange, helping to expand students' perspectives in their programs of study and more broadly as educated citizens working across global contexts.

Alongside these benefits come a number of important questions and considerations that instructors and their institutions must take into account if they are committed to fostering success for international students:

- How can my colleagues and I ensure that our classrooms and campuses are welcoming and inclusive for international students?

- What do I need to know about students' cultural backgrounds in order to help them understand and thrive within U.S. academic culture?

- How can I ensure that the content for my course is comprehensible to students who are still learning English and/or who are generally less familiar with U.S. history, politics, educational systems, and so on?

- How can I design assignments and assessments that measure student learning fairly, while also taking into account the difficulty of doing academic work in an additional language?

- How might I tap into international students' linguistic and cultural backgrounds more intentionally through my curriculum and instruction?

This book is written for college-level instructors working through these very questions. Our aim is to help instructors better understand the backgrounds, needs, and contributions of international students so they can be effective in supporting those students and helping their institutions make the most of what an increasingly global and multilingual student body has to offer.

Defining Our Terms

Throughout this book, *international student* refers to a student who moves to another country (the "host country") for the purpose of pursuing tertiary or higher education (e.g., at a college or university). Some international students spend a single term or a year in the host country; some pursue a degree or other certification, while others continue on for Optional Practical Training, or OPT (see Appendix F for more information about international student visa policies).

Many international students learned English as an additional language[2] and may have done much of their prior education in languages other than English. However, it is worth noting that increasing numbers of international students are attending high schools in the host country (e.g., Institute of International Education, 2017; Zhang-Wu, 2021). (For more information on international student trends, see Sidebar 01, Growth in U.S. International Student Enrollment, 1996–2020.)

We use the term *domestic students* to refer to students who were born and raised in the host country (the United States, in our case) and are attending college or

---

[2] Throughout this text, we use the labels "students who use English as an additional language [EAL]" and "multilingual writers" as alternatives to some of the other labels that have a more deficit orientation, such as "nonnative speakers of English" or "English as a second language [ESL]." See Oropeza et al. (2010) and Tavares (2021b) for more on the impact of labels on international student experiences in higher education.

university alongside international students. This group of domestic students often includes *resident immigrant* students, who may have been born in other countries but attained some or all of their schooling in the host country. This third group straddles the two categories of domestic and international: Resident immigrant students also engage in cultural and linguistic adjustment at our institutions and may have academic needs and challenges similar to those of international students. However, because many immigrant students have had several years or more of schooling in the host country, their needs and experiences may more closely resemble those of domestic students.

Another group of students that does not fit neatly within the two categories of international and domestic students are *global nomads* (sometimes called "third culture kids"), or students who have lived in multiple countries without attaining permanent residency or citizenship—often because of their parents' employment (e.g., Pollock & Van Reken, 2009). Many institutions refer informally to these students as "transnational," since nation of origin as determined by passport may not match their place of long-term residence and schooling.

Finally, it is worth noting that students who are undocumented U.S. residents may be classified as "non-U.S. citizens" and therefore appear on lists of international student admits, but their needs and experiences tend to differ from students who received most or all of their prior education in countries outside the United States.

Although many of the strategies shared in this book are also helpful for supporting certain groups of domestic students—particularly those who have less experience with the U.S. education system and with doing academic coursework in U.S. English—our focus is primarily on nonimmigrant international students. In particular, we are thinking of students who are relatively new to the United States and navigating an unfamiliar culture in addition to developing their proficiency in social and academic English.

Throughout this book, we use the terms *instructors* and *teachers* to refer to the various individuals responsible for classroom instruction at U.S. institutions of higher education. This group includes faculty at various levels, graduate student instructors (teaching assistants), and staff who have teaching or advising responsibilities. We recognize that teaching contexts vary widely across institutions, and we have tried to make this text relevant to a range of instructional situations. While our focus is on the U.S. context, we know that many of the questions and issues addressed in this book are relevant to instructors in other countries as well (e.g., Andrade, 2006; Cena et al., 2021).

Opportunities and Challenges of International Student Enrollment

What do international students gain from enrolling in U.S. higher education institutions? According to international ranking agencies, the majority of top-ranked colleges and universities worldwide are in the United States, with several others in the United Kingdom, Canada, and Australia (e.g., *U.S. News and World*

Report, 2022). The prestige attributed to these institutions has been extended to the countries in which they reside. Earning a degree from an institution in these countries is considered by many international students to be not only an academic and professional achievement but also an indicator of English language proficiency, as well as a marker of social status. Thus, for many international students, studying in the United States or another English-dominant country is the most viable pathway to future success, either in their home countries or on the global job market.

What do U.S. colleges and universities gain from international student enrollment? As we alluded to earlier, there are a number of benefits to having an increasingly international student body. Many institutions see internationalization as a key component of educational excellence; in turn, they view the global representation within the student body as one measure of successful internationalization, alongside other initiatives, such as study abroad programs, branch campuses in other countries, and more globally oriented curricular and cocurricular offerings at the home institution (Buckner, 2019; Childress, 2009). All of these efforts can help increase all students' intercultural competence and prepare them to engage more effectively as global citizens (Knight, 2004; Leask, 2009). Thus, international student recruitment is one means by which institutions can become more globally oriented, while at the same time attracting the "best and brightest" from around the world.

However, institutional excellence is not the only rationale behind international student recruitment. There are often financial incentives as well (Institute of International Education, 2020). With the instability of economies worldwide, as well as reductions in federal and state funding allocations for higher education, many U.S. colleges and universities have come to view international students as a reliable source of supplemental revenue (Singh, 2021). Some experts have found, in fact, that budget shortages are often the *primary* driving force behind increased recruitment efforts (e.g., National Association for College Admissions Counseling, 2013).

This economic incentive can raise concerns about financial exploitation. International students often pay tuition at rates higher than what is paid by out-of-state domestic students (Anderson, 2015; Choudaha, 2020; Marcucci & Johnstone, 2007). They also may be expected to pay additional fees for required language testing or remedial English language classes (e.g., Shapiro, 2012). The false assumption that "all of our international students come from wealthy families" is often used as justification for these sorts of policies. Although international students do not qualify for federal financial aid, they may receive support from institutions or external scholarships. Moreover, some students may be considered "well off" in their home countries, but their families may struggle to afford tuition because currencies and the cost of living vary widely around the world. It is unhelpful—and can even be damaging—to make assumptions about any student's financial background based only on nonimmigrant status.

The reality is that many institutions decide to admit a higher number of international students without articulating a plan for monitoring and supporting that population. This lack of a plan can harm students and creates resentment among faculty and staff, who may feel that they have not been adequately prepared to address the needs of this population, let alone leverage their assets for the benefit of the general student body. As a result, fair treatment of international students is a concern at many institutions, in part because many schools have not addressed the following question: *Whose job is it to ensure that international students have the academic, linguistic, social, and other support they need to be successful?*

This question can only be answered through extensive dialogue and collaborative decision-making at each institution. There are, of course, many entities that play a role in fostering success for our international students. However, for most of this book, we focus on helping instructors understand their role in fostering the success of international students in their classes, which may include working with other campus partners in this endeavor.

This book is thus undergirded by an understanding of the *rights* and *responsibilities* of international students. We believe international students have a right to equitable treatment by their institutions, including nonpunitive policies for admissions and assessment, inclusive practices for teaching and advising, and academic resources and opportunities tailored to their particular needs and goals. Fair treatment also means recognizing that "native-like" English is not a realistic expectation for students who use English as an additional language and that language variation, including a "written accent" in student work, is not necessarily a problem (e.g., Choi, 2016; Harris & Silva, 1993; see more on this topic in Chapter 3). For their part, international students have a responsibility to communicate effectively with instructors and other staff, put in sufficient effort toward reaching their academic goals, and make use of the programs and services designed to support them.

As instructors, we play an important role in ensuring that these rights and responsibilities are understood and honored. Moreover, we can recognize and tap into the assets that accompany an increasingly global, multilingual, and multicultural student body. It is not enough simply to bring a diverse group of students to our campuses and classrooms—we have to set up our curricula and instruction in ways that leverage student diversity to increase student learning. After all, many of the issues and problems our students want to address in their scholarly, professional, and civic lives are global in nature. But as is noted in Buckner et al. (2020), institutions of higher education rarely explicitly articulate the presumed benefits of internationalization or lay out strategic plans for ensuring that they have the systems in place to achieve those benefits.

Our Background and Motivations

All three authors have worked in higher education for a number of years, supporting instructors, staff, and administrators in their work with international students. We have taught in a variety of settings, including public research universities, private liberal arts colleges, intensive English programs, and other

English language classrooms in and outside the United States. We offer courses designed specifically for international students, as well as courses for mixed groups of international and domestic students.

Collectively, we have a broad knowledge base about the beliefs and experiences of instructors, staff, and students, developed through our empirical research (e.g., interviews, surveys, etc.) and through our participation in countless workshops, committees, task forces, and individual consultations. We draw on this knowledge base daily in our collaborations with academic departments, writing programs, writing and learning centers, English language programs, international student resource centers, faculty development programs, and other entities. Over the years, we have observed that there are few books written for U.S. higher education instructors on the topic of international student support. Our aim in writing this book is to present the very best of what we have to offer as teachers, teacher educators, researchers, and consultants—to share the insights, strategies, and resources that our colleagues have found to be most useful.

Our Approach

Building on What Teachers Already Know and Do

There are several key features of our approach to professional development. First, we aim to build on what instructors already know and do. This means that we ask readers to reflect on their past experiences and consider how those experiences inform their pedagogical practices. We aim to cultivate the sorts of "light bulb moments" we see in our day-to-day work, when instructors become aware of how a relatively small choice—such as defining key terms prior to a reading, incorporating more visuals into course lecture, using a small-group format for class discussion, or developing a rubric for writing assessment—can greatly improve academic outcomes for international students. These sorts of choices are generally considered pedagogical "best practices," but they have additional benefits for international students, as they help increase comprehension, lower anxiety, and make expectations more explicit (e.g., Blok et al., 2020).

We know that many instructors already think deeply about their teaching and have likely implemented strategies and activities that are of great benefit to international students. (In fact, many of the ideas we share in this book have come from instructors who are *not* specialists in teaching English to speakers of other languages.) We aim to build on our readers' existing repertoire of successful practices so that they have a deeper understanding of how their pedagogical choices impact the learning experience for international students. In other words, support for international students is not an "add on"; it is part of our commitment to inclusive and equitable teaching for all students.

Drawing on Scholarship of Teaching and Learning

The second feature of our work is that we draw on scholarship of teaching and learning to present the rationale for suggested pedagogical practices. We incorporate concepts from research in applied linguistics, education, composition and writing studies, and intercultural communication as part of the theoretical framework for this book. We pair these concepts with vignettes and examples from instructors and students across disciplines, as well as with reflection questions and other "food for thought." We hope readers will come away with a solid grounding in educational praxis—the intersection of theory, practice, and reflection— regarding their work with international students. We also draw heavily on research in second language acquisition, which provides insights into the challenges that students who use English as an additional language might face in their academic studies, in addition to the contributions that these multilingual learners make to our classrooms and institutions.

We recognize that many different conceptual frameworks are used in scholarship on teaching and learning to talk about effective and ethical pedagogical practices with diverse groups of students. Some of the most prominent frameworks include the following:

- inclusive pedagogy
- antiracist pedagogy
- Universal Design for Learning
- linguistically and culturally responsive teaching and learning
- education for global citizenship
- teaching for social justice

Although each of these frameworks has particular points of emphasis, the pedagogical best practices they support often overlap significantly. There are two particular values that we have found underlie pedagogical best practices for working with linguistically, culturally, and racially diverse groups of students: *access* and *asset*. We have used these concepts elsewhere (e.g., Tomaš & Shapiro, 2021) and found them helpful in framing our commitments to supporting international students and valuing what they bring to our classrooms and institutions.

Access is shorthand for our commitment to expanding opportunities for all students to learn, including international students. Some of the pedagogical strategies that reflect a commitment to access include

- being transparent about our course goals, policies, and procedures;
- offering a range of opportunities for students to learn, review, and apply course skills and concepts;
- creating academic resources and other instructional scaffolding (see Chapter 3) to help all students do their best work;

- using course materials, activities, and assignments that are engaging, relevant, and accessible for students from a variety of backgrounds;

- removing barriers to learning (e.g., psychological, financial, logistical, etc.); and

- understanding how our structures, policies, and resources impact international students, then considering ways to share responsibility for international student support across programs and entities.

Asset refers to our commitment to recognizing and inviting the contributions that international students make to teaching and learning at our institutions. If we see international student recruitment not just as a "numbers game" but as an essential component to the missions of our institutions, then we must advocate for curricula and policies that invite students to bring their whole selves—including their linguistic resources, cultural insights, and global perspectives. We must also avoid institutional policies and practices that are alienating and punitive, as we discuss in Chapter 5. Some of the most common strategies for valuing student assets include

- designing courses centered on global, transnational, and intercultural topics;

- diversifying course readings and other materials to include more global, multilingual, and cross-cultural perspectives;

- crafting assignments that invite students to draw on their background knowledge and lived experiences as transnational and global citizens;

- creating opportunities for students to critique certain aspects of U.S. academic culture and power dynamics in academic disciplines, as well as U.S.-centrism, colonialism, and white supremacy;

- making space for students to use and reference their other linguistic resources in the classroom and on campus (e.g., through opportunities to publish work that uses multiple languages or codes); and

- advocating for institutional policies and practices that recognize multilingualism and global diversity as assets, rather than deficits.

Promoting Equity and Belonging for All Students

Finally, as we alluded to earlier, we know that many of the strategies that are helpful to international students are in fact beneficial for *all* students. In other words, we see international student support as one component of our broader institutional commitments to diversity, equity, inclusion, and access, or DEIA (Carroll & Ryan, 2005; Tavares, 2021a; Wick & Willis, 2020). We are aware that many college instructors have already adapted their classroom pedagogy in numerous ways to respond to the increased racial, cultural, and socioeconomic diversity seen in the student body over the past several decades. We, like many of our colleagues, have also been reflecting in recent years about how to work against racism, xenophobia, ableism, and other forms of injustice, as well as how to promote a sense of belonging and well-being among all of our students. This book thus builds on insights from DEIA scholarship to expand and refine our pedagogical repertoire so we take into account the backgrounds, needs, and assets of international students.

Overview of the Book

Chapter Overview

In this first chapter, we have provided a context and rationale for this volume. Chapter 2 discusses the role of academic culture in the educational experiences of international students and the ways we can support these students' transition into the culture of our classrooms. We provide an overview of key elements of U.S. academic culture, highlighting common practices and expectations that might be unfamiliar to students who were educated in other academic systems. We then provide strategies instructors can employ to help international students understand and adjust to this type of academic culture, including ways to be explicit about expectations, promote interaction in the classroom, and attend to cultural background knowledge that might be important for grasping course material. We conclude with suggestions for promoting cultural inclusion and intercultural competence in our course design, materials, and assignments, citing examples from a variety of disciplines.

In Chapter 3, we shift the focus to language proficiency as a factor in the teaching and learning of international students. After presenting some essential information about language learning and proficiency, we offer a framework of three specific concepts from second language acquisition: *scaffolding*, *interaction*, and *noticing*. We then describe how these concepts can be applied to all aspects of our instruction, including helping students engage with course readings and media, preparing and delivering lectures, and facilitating class discussion. We touch on other aspects of pedagogical decision-making as well and provide suggestions for supporting students as lifelong language learners.

Chapter 4 builds on Chapter 3, examining more closely how we can effectively and equitably measure student learning in our assignments and assessment practices. We first present some definitions and principles that inform best practices for assessment and assignment design, tying those principles back to the values of access and asset. We then consider ways to minimize cultural and linguistic bias and to provide timely and useful feedback on student work. This includes a discussion of considerations related to language use in the writing of students for whom English is an additional language, as well as of fair practices for grading and evaluation of student work. We conclude the chapter by touching on some of the other assessment issues we are often consulted about when it comes to international students, including collaborative work, plagiarism and source use, and special accommodations for exams and other high-stakes assessment.

Chapter 5 focuses on ways to support international students' social and emotional adjustment and to engage in institutional collaboration and advocacy on their behalf. We first explore in more detail some of the ethical considerations related to international student recruitment and support. Then, we discuss how we can support the "whole student" through our advising, community-building, and offerings of support, both individually and with a group. Next, we discuss some of the key entities on our campuses that can be of benefit both to international students and to us in our work with those students. These resources include international student offices, libraries, and writing and learning centers. We then return to the topic of valuing the assets of international students, offering examples of how students' global perspectives, cultural and linguistic backgrounds, and other contributions can be recognized in the classroom and beyond. The final section of this chapter offers suggestions for how we can advocate for equity and inclusion for international students across our institutions.

Within each chapter, we provide pedagogical strategies and activities applicable to content courses in a variety of academic disciplines. We also include sidebars with illustrative quotes from students and instructors, pedagogical examples, instructional scenarios, and reflection questions that reinforce key ideas.

The Afterword includes a list of 10 key strategies, intended as a quick-reference tool to remind readers of some of the most impactful pedagogical insights that appear throughout the book. We also provide a Reading Guide with questions that can support readers' engagement with the text. These questions may also be useful for readers who wish to use this text as part of professional learning with their colleagues or administrators.

The Appendixes and the companion website for this book (www.tesol.org/FISS) provide some of the additional information and resources our faculty colleagues have found most helpful, including the following:

- a handout on international visa policies (new to this edition!)
- an overview of the most commonly used English language proficiency exams (also new!)
- a table with some of our favorite classroom activities (revised for this edition)
- sample grading rubrics from a variety of disciplines
- resources for teaching oral presentations and public speaking
- tips on working with grammar in writing
- an annotated list of journals relevant to international and multilingual student support
- access to online resources connected to the book (www.tesol.org/FISS)

Changes to the Second Edition

In this second edition, we have added a number of important new topics and expanded upon several key existing topics from the first edition. New topics include more information on institutional planning and support structures, including cocurricular offerings (e.g., community-connected learning), and strategies for promoting social and cultural integration. We've added additional information on curricular design and redesign, including options for remote learning and tips for the use of technology. There is also new information on a range of topics related to supporting student learning, including understanding test scores and policies, social-emotional learning, special considerations for STEM instruction, and responding to stereotypes about international students.

This second edition also delves further into several issues around equity: implementing inclusive and asset-based pedagogy, promoting equitable treatment of students, and enacting linguistically responsive and antiracist teaching. We also expand on the topics of responding to plagiarism, providing effective and efficient feedback, and engaging cross-cultural and multilingual perspectives across the curriculum. The Afterword, which contains key insights and strategies and a reading guide, is also a new addition to this book.

We hope that our pragmatic, hands-on orientation throughout this book, along with guidelines and frameworks to support best practices, will help readers internalize the information presented and incorporate what they have learned into their curricula and instruction. We believe readers will come away with a better understanding of the challenges and opportunities presented by an increasingly internationalized student body, as well as insights and strategies that can enhance the learning experience for all students.

CHAPTER 2

Supporting Cultural Adjustment and Inclusion

One of the ways we can promote educational access for international students is to understand how our cultural values and norms might shape our academic expectations and students' educational experiences. Indeed, academic culture shapes many of our expectations about class participation, teacher-student interactions, effective writing, and many other aspects of teaching and learning. By understanding some of the particularities of U.S. academic culture, we can help make our expectations more explicit, which supports students in the cultural adjustment process. Moreover, by treating cultural difference as an asset, rather than a problem, we can help promote intercultural learning and global citizenship for all of the students in our classrooms and on our campuses.

In this chapter, we first provide a brief definition of "culture" in general, then lay out some of the typical values and features of U.S. academic culture that might be unfamiliar or difficult for international students coming from other educational systems. We then present a range of strategies for helping international students adjust to U.S. academic culture, including building community, making expectations explicit, scaffolding student engagement, and reflecting on cultural references. Throughout this discussion, we have woven in reflection questions and quotes from international students for readers to ponder.

What Is "Culture"?

A frog sitting on the bank of a river sees a fish swim by and asks, "How's the water?" The fish looks up and replies, "What water?"

Culture is so much a part of us that we may find it difficult to identify what constitutes our own culture. Like the fish unaware of the water in which it is swimming, we may not recognize our own frames of cultural reference until they are pointed out to us by someone who has a different perspective.

So, what is culture? Most of definitions of the term refer to beliefs, assumptions, norms, attitudes, behaviors, and artifacts that are often tacit but have a strong influence on social interactions. Hammond (2015) uses the metaphor of a tree to reflect the idea that culture, like a tree, is part of a larger ecosystem. In the tree model, the observable fruit reflects the surface culture, which includes food, holidays, dress, and dance. The trunk and branches reflect shallow culture, or unspoken rules related to eye contact, personal space, theories of wellness, and conceptions of time. Surface and shallow culture are taught more frequently in school, mentioned in world language classes, and referenced in travel guides.

02

Reflection Questions About Academic Culture

- What aspects of "deep culture" influence your understanding of what it means to be a good teacher?

- What cultural values have shaped your understanding of academic success and student engagement (e.g., collaboration, competition, etc.)?

- What aspects of U.S. academic culture (or other cultures you work in) are concerning to you? How might you talk about these concerns with students?

Source. Adapted from Hammond (2015).

The grounding root system of the tree captures deep culture, which is the "bedrock of self-concept, group identity, approaches to problem-solving, and decision making" (Hammond, 2015, p. 24). At this level, we find beliefs, norms, and assumptions reflected in our worldview, conceptions of self, definitions of group identity and kinship, notions of fairness, and so on.

Deep culture can significantly influence how we communicate and how we respond to the communicative behaviors of others. When our cultural expectations are violated, this can lead to breakdowns in communication, feelings of embarrassment or withdrawal, or simply a sense of disconnect from those around us. Similarly, when we only view others' actions through our personal cultural frames, we may perpetuate misinterpretations about their actions and intentions. Hammond (2015) invites us to identify aspects of our surface, shallow, and deep culture that may have been hidden to us (see Sidebar 02, Reflection Questions About Academic Culture).

Academic Cultures

When it comes to education, cultural expectations run quite deep, shaping our intuitive responses to questions such as the following: What does learning look like? What does it mean to be a good student? What rhetorical moves does a writer need to make to reach their readers? The following section outlines some of the values that tend to shape U.S. instructors' answers to those questions. Once we "see" these cultural values (i.e., the "water" we are swimming in), we can help explain those values to our students so they can make informed decisions about whether and how they might adjust their own academic behaviors and expectations. Thus, acknowledging cultural expectations is a first step toward ensuring access and success for international students. Sidebar 03, Academic Culture: Common Scenarios, has some common situations in which differences in academic cultures may play a role. We will return to those scenarios later in the chapter.

Before moving on, we wish to point out a few important cautions related to culture. First, it can be dangerous to make decisions based on generalizations about particular groups. If we base our expectations for an individual student only on our knowledge of that student's home country, language, or ethnic group, we may make inaccurate and harmful assumptions. Culturally aware educators are reflective practitioners who take the time to understand their own cultural frames of reference and consider how those frames might shape their perceptions about learners, learner behaviors, and classroom interactions (Hammond, 2015).

Engaging in this sort of self-reflection lessens the likelihood that we will make deficit-based evaluations of our learners. Author and activist Chimamanda Ngozi Adichie (2009) explains this powerfully in her much-loved TED Talk "The Danger of a Single Story." We often show her talk in our classes, in fact, as a way to get students thinking about the intersections of language, culture, and power. Another TED Talk we use to get students thinking about how simple "get to know you" questions might carry cultural assumptions is one by Taiye Selasi (2014) called "Don't Ask Where I'm From, Ask Where I'm a Local."

A second and related caution is that the goal of understanding cultural differences is not to feel a sense of "pity" for international students who have to go through the process of cultural adjustment; rather, the goal is to appreciate the diverse experiences and perspectives students bring to our institutions and to support them in their academic journeys. This distinction is crucial because well-meaning instructors sometimes lower academic expectations or make other harmful decisions in their attempt to "help" international students. Although the cultural adjustment process can be extremely difficult, most international students welcome the challenge. They do not want to be treated as inferior or deficient. They simply need explicit guidance and sustained support in order to meet our high standards. (Questions about "fair treatment" and acceptable accommodations are also discussed in Chapter 4.)

A final reminder is that cultural adjustment needs to be a two-way process: The goal is not blind "assimilation" or eradication of cultural differences. Instead, we want to promote students' engagement across cultural differences so that *all students*, domestic and international, build their intercultural competence, a skill set that many institutions—and many employers—say is crucial today (e.g., Crose, 2011).

Features of U.S. Academic Culture

In the sections that follow, we discuss some of the most prominent values and features of U.S. academic culture. Of course, each institution—and sometimes an

Academic Culture: Common Scenarios

Have you experienced scenarios similar to those described below? If so, what steps did you take (or could you take) to address these behaviors or at least understand why they were happening?

Scenario 1: One instructor noted that some of her international students appeared reluctant to share much in groups with their peers and rarely contributed to whole-class discussions. She wanted to know what she could do to involve them without putting them on the spot.

Scenario 2: An instructor noticed that the essays from some international students tended to lack in-text citations. When he discussed the issue with students, they did not seem to understand why it was a major problem.

Scenario 3: An instructor who likes to incorporate class presentations noted that one student always apologized at the start of her presentation, making statements such as "I know my English isn't that good, so I hope you will understand me." This surprised the teacher because she believed the student's proficiency in English to be quite high.

individual program or department—has its own subculture. But there are some aspects of U.S. academic culture that tend to shape norms and expectations across disciplines. After we discuss these aspects, we will turn to strategies for supporting cultural adjustment for international students and promoting intercultural engagement for everyone.

Individualism

One important dimension of culture that permeates the literature on intercultural communication is the extent to which given cultures embrace individualism or collectivism (e.g., Triandis, 2001). Collectivist societies place an emphasis on closer relationships, cooperation, group decision-making, willingness to accept the views of others, and concern for saving face and gaining the approval of the collective. In contrast, individualist societies such as the United States are characterized by competition, self-reliance, independence, and the rejection of arbitrary authority in favor of equality (Bellah et al., 2007; Triandis, 1993). Of course, no community is strictly individualist or collectivist: These orientations tend to play out differently in various parts of society. However, the value of individualism does shape many aspects of U.S. higher education.

One manifestation of individualism in U.S. academic culture is the heavy focus on individual *voice* in class discussion and in students' written work (Ramanathan & Atkinson, 1999). U.S. students are often expected to develop and express their "own" ideas about course material—even if they have only been learning about a topic for a matter of weeks! Although some faculty use other formats to encourage more collaboration and idea-sharing, as we will discuss, "participation" in class is usually measured in terms of each individual's frequency of speaking in class. This means that in many class discussions in the United States, students are rewarded more for speaking than for listening. (We discuss this further in this chapter and in Chapters 3 and 4.) Students accustomed to other academic cultures, in contrast, may have been taught to listen for a long time before speaking or to see the instructor as the sole authority on course content—or perhaps both. Assuming authority to speak may strike these students as presumptuous and arrogant, as it undervalues expertise and collective (versus individual) knowledge.

Given this divergence in academic cultural expectations, it is unsurprising that many international students find it difficult to join in class discussions, even if they know they are expected to speak early and often. This is probably what is happening in Scenario 1 in Sidebar 03. And of course, those who struggle with the linguistic demands of academic listening and speaking have additional hurdles as well, which is why scaffolding student participation—a strategy we will discuss later in this chapter and in Chapter 3—is so helpful for international students, as well as with domestic students who might find it difficult to speak in a large-group discussion.

Intellectual Ownership

A related manifestation of individualism in U.S. higher education is a strong belief in the concept of intellectual ownership. Words and ideas are thought of as "belonging" to individual people, and if a U.S. student wants to reference them, they are expected to use the appropriate "textual borrowing" practices (e.g., paraphrase, citation, etc.). This idea can be quite confusing, causing students to wonder, "How am I supposed to know whether my words or ideas might have been influenced by something I read or heard years ago?" And because academic English has many frequently used groupings or collocations (e.g., "These findings have important implications" or "One limitation of the current study is …"), how can students know which clauses are plagiarized and from where?

These are high-stakes questions, of course, because using someone else's words or ideas without correct attribution (i.e., plagiarism) is treated as a type of stealing at most U.S. institutions and may therefore result in serious consequences. As we will explore further in Chapter 4, this notion of intellectual ownership may be quite different in other academic cultures. Thus, international students often need explicit information and instruction on how to integrate and draw from other sources in their academic work (e.g., Tomaš & Shapiro, 2021). This insight helps us understand what is happening in Scenario 2 in Sidebar 03.

Initiative and Assertiveness

Individualistic tendencies also influence the level of initiative and assertiveness expected from students. When U.S. students are struggling academically, they are encouraged to seek help or advice from the instructor or to search for more information from other sources. However, in some academic cultures, asking for one-on-one help from an instructor could be seen as presumptuous—or even a challenge to their expertise as teachers (Mendelsohn, 2002; see later in this chapter and Chapter 5 for additional strategies for encouraging help-seeking). Assertiveness also plays into "argument culture" (Tannen, 2013), in which many scholarly and political discussions are seen as "battles" in which participants must "take a position" and "defend" it against counterarguments. This dynamic once again prioritizes speaking over listening and promotes division rather than consensus. Participating in such a culture can be particularly difficult for students who come from communities where open criticism of authorities is discouraged or even actively suppressed.

The value of assertiveness also plays out in expectations for oral presentations, applications for jobs and internships, and professional interviews. In these situations, students are often expected to present an aura of confidence, emphasizing their strengths and deemphasizing weaknesses. Even if they feel they may not be the most prepared or qualified candidate, U.S. students are often encouraged to "fake it till you make it." In many other academic or professional cultures, candidates are expected to do almost the opposite, exuding humility rather than confidence (e.g., Li, 2016). Even if they feel well prepared and qualified, students in those settings may be encouraged to downplay their own accomplishments and abilities, as a way to show respect for authority and consideration for the collective over the individual. The key insight is that a student may be equally skilled in spite of whether they are "performing" confidence or humility in a particular situation. Performed humility may in fact be the reason for the student behavior in Scenario 3 in Sidebar 03.

Indeed, one of the cultural values that is the most difficult for many U.S. students (and teachers as well!) to understand is the idea of saving face (e.g., Ting-Toomey & Oetzel, 2002; see Sidebar 04, Student Perspectives on Instructor Interactions). In many cultures—especially in academic or professional situations—one might use indirectness, omission of details, or even a "polite lie" to avoid awkwardness or public embarrassment. This face-saving strategy is usually understood as such by both people involved. For example, someone might reply "maybe" to an invitation to a presentation or gathering, knowing full well that they will not attend. Saving face may be another reason that some international students are at times reluctant to ask for clarification on a concept or support for an assignment, as these admissions might inadvertently imply that their instructor has failed in some way.

Academic Choices

Another way in which individualism is expressed in U.S. higher education is in the range of academic choices given to U.S. students. At many U.S. institutions, students have a great deal of autonomy in choosing their courses and programs of study; they may also have a lot of leeway in choosing topics for research projects or other assignments. Many international students, in contrast, are used to a more structured approach (see Sidebar 04). Though they often find the freedom of choice at U.S. institutions refreshing, international students may also feel overwhelmed by the range of options and might need guidance and support to make appropriate choices. Moreover, having so much choice makes it unlikely that students will be in more than one class with any of their peers, which can make it difficult for students to build social connections in class, unless their institution forms intentional cohorts or learning communities (e.g., Rocconi, 2011).

The value of individualism also impacts the social scene on U.S. campuses. Some international students are surprised by how infrequently they have opportunities to chat informally with their peers. They show up at dining halls and see other students sitting alone, scrolling on phones as they eat. Students head back to their living spaces and are surprised by the empty hallways and closed doors. Of course, institutions usually provide cocurricular and extracurricular programming for students looking to build and strengthen friendships outside the classroom. However, opportunities for organic and casual conversation are rarer than many instructors realize. Once again, students are expected to take initiative if they want to build a network of friends. This is one reason why it is valuable to build community in class and to promote frequent interactions and collaboration, as will be explored further in this chapter, as well as in Chapters 3 and 4.

04

Student Perspectives on Instructor Interactions

"I was too ashamed to ask for help. I didn't think I deserved it. I'm so glad my professor reached out to me."
—Student from Mexico

"I think that encouraging international students to meet instructors individually helps students to open up and talk more about problems that they are facing in the classroom."
—Student from China

"Students can have much freedom in their study, in terms of subject and research interest. It is quite different [from] mentorship in China, [where] students are told by the adviser to do which type of research in which field and using which specific methods. I try to adapt to the mentorship in the United States but still have difficulty."
—Student from China

Creativity and Innovation

Related to the value of individualism is the emphasis on creativity and innovation, rather than memorization and recall of facts, in most U.S. schools. Being able to express "original" ideas and craft "new" arguments is seen as a key academic skill and a prerequisite for success in U.S. higher education. On exams and assignments, many instructors expect students to not only summarize course material but also offer a personal opinion or critical perspective. Some U.S. instructors even encourage students to disagree with the instructor or other established authorities on a topic. Although some international students enjoy this challenge, many feel uncomfortable questioning the instructor's authority.

The reality is that an "original contribution" can be defined in a variety of ways, depending on the assignment and discipline. In their article on working with faculty to promote effective source use strategies among students, Tomaš and Shapiro (2021) provide some examples of "what 'being original' actually means" (p. 5), drawn from conversations and workshops with faculty across disciplines. These examples include

- synthesis of information,

- demonstrations and applications of theories or concepts,

- critiques or extensions of an argument, and

- connections between course learning and other disciplines and communities.

For the original article by Tomaš and Shapiro, visit the companion website for this book (www.tesol.org/FISS). See Mott-Smith et al. (2017) for more on this topic, as well as Sidebar 05, Student Perspectives on Classroom Culture.

Informality in the Classroom

Another key aspect of academic and professional culture we have alluded to is what Hofstede et al. (2010) call "power distance" —that is, the amount of deference given to authority figures. Students from countries with higher power distance are often surprised by the less-hierarchical relationship between teachers and students in the United States. For example, in many countries, a student would never call a teacher by their first name, but this is common practice at many U.S. colleges and universities. International students may additionally be surprised to find students and instructors having closer physical contact (e.g., hugging) than they are used to or interacting socially outside the classroom. These differing understandings can affect simple classroom behaviors, such as whether students can go to the bathroom without first getting permission from the instructor or whether they should knock on the door to enter if they are late to class. In other words, in many academic cultures, informality is perceived as disrespect.

The classroom environment at U.S. institutions also strikes many international students as relatively informal. In some countries, students tend to dress professionally for school, as if they were going to work. In the United States, in contrast, students usually wear street clothes, and we have even had students show up in pajamas or bathrobes! International students may find it strange to see instructors dressing casually themselves or showing relaxed postures in the classroom, such as sitting on the edge of a desk. Misunderstanding could arise here, as students may misinterpret this casual, informal behavior as an indication that the course itself will be slower paced or less rigorous, which is not necessarily the case.

This is not to say that a hierarchy between teachers and students is absent at U.S. institutions. Many instructors are surprised when international students ask them personal questions (e.g., "Are you married?") that are seen as acceptable in other cultural contexts. U.S. instructors may also be bothered when students ask about their predicted grade in a class, although this sort of question is also seen as acceptable in other academic cultures. (Later in this chapter, we will provide some strategies for establishing expectations for communication, as a way to prevent some of these misunderstandings.)

Efficiency and Directness

A common saying in U.S. society is "time is money." This idea, which some experts trace to the influence of capitalism (e.g., Kuriyama, 2002), permeates many aspects of U.S. academic culture, including expectations for arriving to class on time, keeping oral presentations short and succinct, and being concise in written work. If students visit an instructor, for example, they are expected to be fairly direct in stating the purpose of their visit.

This value for "efficiency" also influences expectations for academic writing and speaking at U.S. institutions. Students are usually expected to present their main ideas early and make sure that each point is explicitly connected to their key ideas. In writing, they are usually expected to prioritize clarity and conciseness in their use of language in order to make the writing easier for the reader to digest. These patterns differ from the norm in languages such as Chinese, in which it is often considered more appropriate to work gradually toward the main point, rather than stating it up front, or Spanish and Russian, in which scholars are encouraged to use longer, more complex sentences and to tolerate more divergence from the main topic (e.g., Connor, 1996; Kubota & Lehner, 2004). See Sidebar 06, Student Perspectives on Writing in U.S. Academic Culture, for student comments about these cultural differences in writing.

06

Student Perspectives on Writing in U.S. Academic Culture

"In Japanese writing ... readers are supposed to participate [in] the story much more than American writing. And there are so many pronouns but this is the reader's job to understand what this he is and what this she is and what this it refers to. [In] American writing, writers have a lot of [this] responsibility."

"In Ecuador, what we ... sometimes tend to do is that we don't present the main point at the beginning. We go around it and around it until we finally get to the point, which is in the middle. It's kind of like this idea of circularity."

"In Turkish, what we do is we use long and elaborate sentences because we think that it's more poetic and it flows better that way, and you read it for the sake of getting some kind of a pleasure out of it, not necessarily just to understand the point."

These differences in rhetorical expectations often cause U.S. instructors to view international students' writing or oral presentations as illogical or disorganized. They may think that grammatical errors are to blame, not realizing that there are academic cultural values shaping their very conception of "clear writing." Insights like these come from the field of contrastive rhetoric, which studies how arguments are made differently depending on linguistic and cultural context (Connor, 1996; Kubota & Lehner, 2004). Examples of how contrastive rhetoric plays out can be seen in the documentary *Writing Across Borders* (Burton et al., 2005), which is the source of the quotes in Sidebar 06. (See also Sidebar 07, An Email Not Meeting Expectations for Efficiency in Writing, for an example of student writing that did not fit with the instructor's expectations.)

By understanding how academic culture shapes our expectations as readers and listeners, we can be more effective in our feedback to students. We can even open up critical conversations about the downsides of certain aspects of U.S. academic culture. We might ask students, for example, "What are the dangers of prioritizing efficiency over sophistication or complexity in writing?" or "What genres of writing and speaking do not lend themselves well to an emphasis on conciseness or linearity?" Such conversations help deepen all students' understandings about the relationship between language, culture, and power (Kubota & Lehner, 2004; Shapiro, 2022). We will return to several of these points in Chapter 4 in our discussion of assignments and assessments, including evaluating student work.

07

An Email Not Meeting Expectations for Efficiency in Writing

Where is the main point of the student's request in the email below? In what ways might the writing in this email diverge from what is typically expected in U.S. academic culture?

> Dear Respected Professor XXX,
>
> I would like to tell you that, good chance comes only once in the life. I am a foreign student come from oversee to educate myself and challenge myself. I came here with all hope and excitement to study. I am a mother and I am working. My position will be held for me for 2 years and if there is any delay with my studying I will not be able to have my job again. Women in my country don't have chance to be creative she has to fight and not give up. These day your education is your support and without that I will be weak. I am nothing even if I have a lot of money my brain will be empty. Thank you for reading my letter and your understanding and I hope I will be allowed into this course.
>
> Regards, Xxxxx

Source. Reprinted with permission from Tomaš et al. (2020).

Other Key Characteristics of U.S. Classrooms

There are a few other features of U.S. higher education that are worth noting as points of distinction from many other academic cultures.

Demographic Diversity

Some international students come from countries where the student demographics are more homogeneous than in the United States in terms of age,

08

Dealing With Difficult Classroom Scenarios

Scenario A: Students from countries or regions that have been in conflict (e.g., Taiwan and mainland China) begin arguing about politics during class discussion.

Option 1: Redirect students back to the main topic of the conversation if the conflict is not directly relevant to the topic at hand.

Option 2: Encourage students to reference the conflict in their writing or other work for class, if appropriate, but remind them to think carefully about their audience and to reference a variety of perspectives on the issue.

Scenario B: A student from a culture (or community) where male and female students are usually educated separately (e.g., Saudi Arabia) asks to be exempted from mixed-gender interactions during class

Option 1: Ask the student for more information about what aspects of mixed-gender interactions are inappropriate. In many cases, physical contact is a greater concern than verbal interaction and can be avoided.

Option 2: Develop a plan for which classroom activities require mixed-gender interaction and which do not (e.g., perhaps the student needs to participate in mixed groups during class but could be allowed to work with a same-gender partner for out-of-class assignments).

Scenario C: Two international students from the same country have submitted work that is quite similar for an assignment that is supposed to be completed individually. When asked about this similarity, the students seem confused, as they had thought collaboration was encouraged.

Option 1: After clarifying with students, revise assignment instructions to be clear about when and how collaboration might be used.

Option 2: Allow students to collaborate by request on some aspects of the assignment (e.g., analysis) but require an individual write-up from each student.

Option 3: Invite all students to work with a partner on some assignments, with opportunities to provide feedback from time to time on how the collaboration is going.

race, ethnicity, socioeconomic class, gender, and sexual orientation. For example, in some countries, nearly all university students are recent high school graduates, and their professors tend to be from the same ethnic background. Consequently, students coming to the United States from these settings may be surprised to be learning alongside older or returning students who may already have years of work experience and being taught by instructors from across the United States and around the world.

Range of Course Types, Formats, and Expectations

International students may also be less familiar with the variety of course formats used in U.S. higher education, which encompasses not just lecture-style courses, but also discussion sections, recitations, seminars, labs, studios, and online or hybrid courses. Instructors who are advising international students in course selection may need to take extra time to explain each of these formats, as may be necessary with other groups, such as first-generation college students.

There has been a shift in U.S. education toward more learner-centered models of instruction, in which the instructor is a facilitator of active learning, rather than the sole provider of information or what some call "sage on a stage" (e.g., Nilson, 2010; Weimer, 2013). One iteration of this learner-centered approach is "flipped" instruction, in which students first encounter new material outside the classroom, through readings and/or recorded lectures, then build on that knowledge through group activities in class (see Chapter 3 for more on this topic). For example, many instructors often invite or require students to take part of the responsibility for teaching—for example, by having them explain course concepts or facilitate discussion around a reading. Taking on this responsibility can be intimidating for students who have never been asked to do anything like this before. Providing clear guidelines, models, and scaffolding can be of tremendous benefit to students making this particular cultural adjustment.

Another increasingly common trend is to include service learning or other community engagement as part of a course. This is a way to deepen student learning, align academic goals with community assets and needs, and build students' skills for employment and ethical citizenship (e.g., Lindahl et al., 2018; Tomaš et al., 2020). Although service learning often takes place in the local community, there has been a rise in virtual exchange programs that work across geographic contexts in recent years (O'Dowd, 2021). It is worth noting that the concept of community service and volunteering itself is something that differs across cultural contexts: In many countries, governmental organizations are responsible for much of the work that is done by nongovernmental organizations and volunteers in the United States. Faculty using community engagement need to make sure goals and expectations are clear, and they may wish to solicit mentors who have engaged in these projects in preceding semesters (see Chapter 5 for more on promoting community-connected learning).

Assessment practices have also been diversified somewhat in recent years at U.S. colleges and universities. Whereas it is not uncommon in some countries for most of a course grade to depend on a cumulative exam (written or oral) at the end of the term, most courses at U.S. institutions include assignments and other assessments that "count" throughout the term. This means that international students may need scaffolding and other strategies to help them adjust to having a steady workload throughout the semester. Many U.S. instructors have also begun to experiment with alternative approaches to grading, such as contract grading (e.g., Danielewicz & Elbow, 2009). These approaches, which take labor, growth, and reflection into account, often benefit international students, but they can be baffling or anxiety-producing to students who are encountering them for the first time. (See Chapter 4 for a deeper dive into these issues.)

A final shift taking place has to do with the increased emphasis on diversity, equity, inclusion, and access in higher education. Many common classroom practices, such as introducing one's personal pronouns or reading a land acknowledgment statement at the beginning of class, are unfamiliar to international students and may cause confusion if these practices are not explained clearly, as part of our transparency about U.S. academic culture. As is the case with domestic students, faculty should also expect that international students have a wide range of values and awareness of key social issues. As Kubota (2021) argues in her discussion of antiracism work, faculty need to strive for a "delicate balance" that is "anti-oppressive" but also "noncoercive and contextualized" (p. 245). We have worked with international students who were more socially or politically conservative, as well as many who experienced our institutions as overly conservative or even oppressive. This complexity once again points to the importance of self-reflection in thinking through when and how we address social, political, and cultural issues in the classroom.

We hope that this discussion of academic cultural values, practices, and trends helps instructors "see" their academic cultures more clearly and offer a clear rationale for what they do in their classrooms and curricula and why. The remainder of this chapter is devoted to discussing how we can support international students' adjustment to U.S. academic culture and tap into cultural difference as an asset for everyone's learning.

Supporting Students' Transition Into U.S. Academic Culture

Although each international student's transition into U.S. academic culture is unique, there are typical patterns in the trajectory. These patterns are often experienced as well by U.S. students who study abroad. Initially, many international students experience a "honeymoon period," characterized by high energy, curiosity, appreciation, and even euphoria (Lee & Rice, 2007; Li & Kaye, 1998). This phase is often followed by a period of disorientation, irritability, or even hostility, referred to colloquially as "culture shock." This is a point at which many students begin to miss the familiarities of home—such as people, food, and housing arrangements—and may start to be critical of the new academic culture to which they are adjusting (Cena et al., 2021; Hirai et al., 2015). During this time, students may struggle to balance their social, academic, and other commitments. They may be more prone to self-isolation, both because of mental health struggles and because this phase often occurs at the same time that academic workload is intensifying (e.g., midterm exams, major assignments due). This stage can be particularly challenging for students for whom English is an additional language, who may struggle to find the time necessary to complete academic work, as will be discussed further in Chapter 3.

Most students eventually enter a phase of gradual adaptation and stability, whereby they develop emotional, social, and logistical coping strategies that allow them to navigate the complexities of the academic and institutional cultures. However, as they take on new experiences and challenges, international students may have recurring periods of destabilization and readjustment. For this reason, some scholars suggest that cultural adjustment is a cyclical rather than linear process (e.g., Heng, 2018).

Of course, we cannot assume that all international students will experience all of these phases. Some international students have had experience with U.S. secondary schools, which can ease their adjustment into higher education (e.g., Zhang-Wu, 2021). Or they may have attended international schools whose academic culture is similar to what we have described. Nonetheless, it is important to be aware that many international students do experience these kinds of struggles and that the greatest challenges may emerge after the initial period of adjustment for domestic students (Andrade, 2006; Brunsting et al., 2018; Shu et al., 2020). There are a number of ways we can support international students' adjustment to U.S. academic culture, and these strategies are often of help to other groups as well, including those who are the first in their families to attend institutions of higher education.

Be Explicit About Your Own Expectations

Another way we can serve as cultural informants for students is to be explicit about our course assumptions, expectations, and requirements early in the semester. Here are some of the points we might touch on in syllabi, handouts, and conversations with students:

Prior Learning

We should be clear from Day 1 about the background knowledge we expect our students to have to be successful in our classes. Even if there are no prerequisites for our courses, we often assume students have had exposure to particular topics or practice with a set of skills. One way to learn more about what students are bringing with them is to do an informal assessment task in the first week of class, such as a writing sample or a survey of past skills and experiences (e.g., "Please tell me what kinds of laboratory equipment you have used before.").

It is also helpful to create a set of online or print resources that students can reference to fill in any gaps in their knowledge base—for example, a glossary of key terminology, a video tutorial, or a model of the kinds of work students will be doing. Such resources can also be useful in courses that assume students have specific cultural information that would be less familiar to international students, such as about U.S. television or film, history or politics, or canonical literature. (We will return to the topic of cultural background knowledge later in this chapter.)

Classroom Behavior

Because classroom expectations vary across academic cultures, it is helpful to give students specific information about what we see as appropriate and effective behavior during class. For example, we can define what "class participation" means for our particular course: Do we count attendance? Are students required to speak during large-group discussions, and how frequently? Are there other opportunities for discussion, such as pair or small-group or online discussions? Does active listening factor in, and what does it look like?

Many instructors factor a wide range of other behaviors into their participation grades as well. These behaviors can include active engagement during in-class activities (e.g., free-writes, simulations, pair or small-group tasks, peer review), timely submission of assignment drafts, use of support resources (e.g., tutors, study group facilitators, course management systems), and attendance at cocurricular events or individual meetings. Stating explicitly what "counts" toward the grade—and of course to student learning—helps us ensure students' successful engagement. Moreover, broadening our conception of what "participation" is can actually make our courses more equitable and inclusive of students from diverse backgrounds. (See Appendix E for a more complete list of behaviors that we can count as participation.)

Communication Norms and Preferences

"Culture" and "communication" are so closely linked that it is important to articulate our communication expectations and preferences to students. In our syllabi or early classes, we should tell them how we prefer to be addressed (e.g., Professor X, Mr./Ms./Mx. X, by first name, or another title). Even if we are comfortable with a variety of terms of address, students appreciate knowing our preferences, as well as what is "typical" at our institutions (or in our particular programs or departments). We should also discuss when and how students might connect with us outside of class. In many academic cultures, office hours are uncommon, so highlighting what they are for and how they work—particularly that students do not need to have an immediate problem or concern in order to stop by—is useful.

We should also be clear about when and how we will communicate with students. Some instructors want all communication to take place via a course management system, while others prefer email or even provide cell phone or chat information. We also tell students that we try to respond to all emails within a set timeframe (e.g., 48 hours), and we expect the same from them.

Teaching Philosophy

Because academic cultures vary widely, as was discussed earlier, many international students appreciate hearing from us about our teaching philosophy. This helps create "buy in" from students who might be resistant to approaches that differ from those familiar to them (e.g., frequent use of group work or simulations, a "flipped classroom" model, or an alternative approach to grading). As we share what students can expect, we can also explain why we have set things up in this way. (We will say more on this in Chapters 3 and 4.) We build a positive class rapport by giving students a window into how we think about our work as educators.

It is also useful—and helpful in community-building—to gather information from students about their experiences and preferences as learners. We may ask students to complete a short free-write early in the course on the question "What would you like me to know about you?" This question often prompts students to share valuable information (of their choosing) about their personal backgrounds; educational histories; and academic goals, strengths, and challenges. Many of the other activities we discuss in this chapter can help instructors elicit this sort of information from students.

Academic Integrity

Students need explicit information as well about academic honesty. Each institution or program may have distinct policies about collaborative work, use of academic supports (e.g., writing and learning centers), test proctoring, and accusations of cheating or other inappropriate behaviors. Plagiarism is another issue for which policies and processes vary widely—even from one instructor to the next (Pecorari & Shaw, 2012); hence, students need explicit guidance on how to recognize plagiarism, as well as explicit instruction and resources for using sources effectively (Mott-Smith et al., 2017; Tomaš & Shapiro, 2021). Instructors may need to return to this particular topic throughout the semester because it is so culturally unfamiliar to students from non-U.S. education systems. (See Chapters 3 and 4 for more on this topic.)

Support and Help-Seeking

Given some of the differences in academic cultures noted earlier (e.g., in the sidebars with student perspectives), it is valuable to explain explicitly to students when, why, and how they can seek academic support (Owen, 2020). Moreover, we can proactively elicit feedback and offer support even before students know they need it! Strategies for doing so include

- requiring short get-to-know-you meetings with us at the beginning of the semester;

- doing short reflections during class (e.g., via free-write) to see what students are struggling with in a unit or on an assignment;

- checking in individually with students as soon as we notice them falling behind (more on this in Chapter 5); and

- highlighting aspects of the course where students typically struggle, and providing strategies and resources in advance.

Other Classroom Policies

Some other policies that students need to know about include attendance, tardiness, illness or emergencies, extensions or late work, and technology in the classroom. Keep in mind, again, that your policies may differ from those of other instructors, which can be confusing to students. Providing explicit information is part of a universal and inclusive approach that benefits everyone!

Be Intentional About Building Community

Many of us aspire to cultivate a sense of belonging in our classrooms, and this is something that today's students say is particularly important to them (Strayhorn, 2018). Although many of us do introductions and "icebreaker" activities in the first session or week, we may forget to continue building community throughout the semester, when students' workloads and stress may threaten their sense of belonging in our classes and at our institutions. International students tend to be particularly appreciative of opportunities to connect with their peers during class—not only for the academic benefit but also because those connections help with social adjustment. Community-building also establishes trusting, respectful relationships, which we can draw on when addressing challenging situations (see Sidebar 08, Dealing With Difficult Classroom Scenarios).

One simple way to start building community is by learning students' names as soon as possible (Zhang & Noels, 2021). Colleagues sometimes ask us whether it is upsetting to international students if we do not know how to pronounce their names or we struggle to learn the correct pronunciation. The truth is that many international students are quite used to teaching the correct pronunciation to others by the time they enter our classes, so they usually take it in stride. It is perfectly acceptable to ask a student how to pronounce their name—and even to repeat it a few times if necessary. This is preferable to trying to make an attempt based only on the written version, or asking students to use an Anglicized alternative, which is not culturally appropriate. (See Sidebar 09, Tips

---

09

Tips for Pronouncing Unfamiliar Names

1. Take notes on your class roster to help you to remember the pronunciation next time (e.g., *"Wang" rhymes with "strong"; "X" in "Xue" makes a "sh" sound*).

2. Remember that for most names, it is relatively easy to find pronunciations online. Simply search for the name and the word "pronunciation" and an audio file will usually appear in the search results. There are a number of databases of audio files for names by region, such as this one: https://pronounce.voanews.com/.

3. Note that many universities have created resources for instructors looking to learn how to pronounce Chinese names in particular. For examples of these resources, visit the companion website for this book (www.tesol.org/FISS).

---

for Pronouncing Unfamiliar Names, for a few additional tips.) It can be a nice community-building opportunity (and a chance to tap into cultural assets) to invite all students to share whether there is a meaning or story behind their names. (For a video of students demonstrating this activity, visit the companion website for this book at www.tesol.org/FISS.)

It is helpful to use name tags or trifold name plates so that everyone has a reminder when needed. Also, there may be tools we can use to help us start learning names even before class starts: Many institutions now have an option for embedding one's name pronunciation as an audio file in administrative databases (e.g., Banner), online learning management systems (e.g., Canvas), and email signatures. We can ask students to add the pronunciation into the system before the course starts or during the first week of class.

In addition to learning names, we should aim to have students interact early and often during class. Below are some strategies and activities we use early in the term, some of which can be repeated throughout the semester.

- **Flip introductions.** Before the start of the semester, one of the authors, Raichle, creates an introduction prompt using Flip (www.flip.com). Students post videos responding to the prompt, then share a reaction to some of their peers' videos. This activity provides students an opportunity to put names to faces and find common interests. The prompt can ask about reasons for taking the course, experience with the course content or topics, goals for the academic year, or personal interests.

- **Syllabus quiz.** After having an opportunity to read over the syllabus at home, students collaborate on a syllabus quiz where they have to try to recollect key information. This quiz gives students an additional incentive for reading closely, as well as an opportunity to clarify with group members. Online tools such as Kahoot! (kahoot.it/) can be useful for this activity.

- **Peer-to-peer interviews.** Students form pairs or small groups to learn more about one another by responding to prompts (e.g., "Find four things you and your partner have in common" or "Talk about your past experiences with this course topic"). Findings can be shared orally with the entire class or in writing through a class discussion forum.

- **"Mix and mingle" activities.** For this kind of activity, students mill about the classroom asking a single question of as many of their peers as possible. For example, one student's assigned question might be "What drew you to this course topic?" (See more sample questions in Chapter 5, Sidebar 39, Jigsaw Survey.) Afterward, students can share a few highlights from the responses they collected with the larger group. (Note: Students will not have the opportunity to interview everyone; we usually encourage them to interview at least five classmates.)

- **People bingo.** This is another mix-and-mingle activity, in which students try to find classmates to match criteria laid out on a bingo card (see Figure 2.1 for an example).

- **Circle share.** Students are given a thought-provoking question to reflect on, ideally one that invites them to tell a personal story. Each student then has the opportunity to share without interruption for 1 to 2 minutes, or students have the option to "pass" if they wish. (See Shapiro, 2022, for more on this activity.)

- **"Pods" or study groups.** Put students into groups for in-class work, and encourage them to share contact information so they can be of support for their peers out of class as well.

- **"Take my advice."** Working in groups, students read five pieces of advice collected by the instructor from former students about the course they are currently taking (or about a specific reading or assignment). They rank the advice from the most to the least helpful and important. This activity provides a personalized, big-picture view of key course issues and helps with community-building. Students can also work in groups throughout the semester to provide academic tips and resources for each other.

- **"The best class ever."** Students are given time to free-write about some of the features they have appreciated in past classes, then work in groups to compile a list of common characteristics.

Figure 2.1 *Sample People Bingo Card, From a First-Year Writing Course*

Instructions: Talk with classmates to find someone who meets each of the criteria in the bingo card. After completing one full row, have a seat and be prepared to share what you learned.

Can explain coherence and/or cohesion	Can define plagiarism	Can list three tips for avoiding plagiarism	Can explain the purpose of a conclusion paragraph
Can list four transition words that might be used to compare and contrast concepts	Can compare argumentation in the United States to academic argumentation in another cultural or rhetorical context	Can explain the function of paragraphs in U.S. academic writing	Can explain how to write an in-text citation from a book using MLA format
Can explain the usefulness of an outline for writing a paper	Can give their opinion about peer feedback	Can explain their revision process for a paper	Can identify three campus resources to help me with writing
Can explain one strategy for integrating information from a source with one's own commentary	Can explain the difference between skimming and scanning	Can explain why Google is not the best tool for academic research	Can explain when to use a direct quote versus when to paraphrase

Be an Academic Cultural Informant

Instructors can serve as "cultural informants" for their students by being explicit about the values, norms, and expectations that students are likely to encounter at their institutions more broadly. This helps students see more clearly the nature of academic culture, which in turn allows them to navigate that culture with greater confidence. Some of the norms that we sometimes forget to explain to students can be addressed by answering the following questions:

- Why do we hand out syllabi on the first day? (Some instructors see a syllabus as a "contract" for the course, for example, but they may not tell students this.)

- Why do we have office hours, and how can students make use of them?

- What is the purpose of a course management system, and how does it contribute to students' learning and assessment?

- When and how can students ask for help (e.g., clarifications of course concepts and materials, extensions on assignments, support from a peer or tutor, or another resource that would support their course learning)? See Chapters 4 and 5 for more on accommodations and support.

- What are some of the downsides of U.S. academic culture? When might there be opportunities for instructors and students to "push back" against cultural norms with which we disagree?

Being an informant also means providing clear feedback on what might be perceived as culturally appropriate or inappropriate. We have found that our colleagues are sometimes hesitant to provide corrective feedback to students who are not following expected cultural norms. For example, they may be annoyed when a student uses a generic title (e.g., "Teacher") rather than referring to them by name (though the generic title is a sign of respect in many academic cultures). Although none of us enjoy awkward conversations, we have found it rewarding to see students' appreciation when we make them aware of a cultural norm that they may not have known. Table 2.1 provides some examples of norms that were unfamiliar to some of our international students.

Table 2.1 *Explanations of Cultural Norms in Response to Student Behaviors*

There are cultural norms that affect written communication as well, which we discussed earlier. Some students are unsure about the norms for particular

Student behavior	Explanation in terms of cultural norms
Apologizing for "bad English" or poor quality work, even in instances when this does not seem to be the case; down-playing or dismissing a compliment	A student's cultural value of humility may not be recognized as important, leaving an instructor puzzled why a student would apologize or dismiss positive feedback.
Talking to an instructor after class without asking whether the instructor has the time to talk outside of office hours	A student may not understand "efficiency" as a cultural value in the U.S. academic context and that expecting unscheduled conversations could be seen as disrespectful.
Asking personal questions about marriage/relationship status, salary, religion, and other personal topics in office hours or other interactions	A student may have a divergent cultural understanding of questions appropriate for casual conversation.
Including copied text from a professor's publication or lecture in the student's own writing without conventional acknowledgment	A student's value of respect for expertise may be at odds with the conception in U.S. education that ideas are commodities that can be owned. The student might have expected the professor to be pleased, or even flattered, instead of hurt or insulted.

genres of writing, such as email, and therefore may come across as overly formal or informal, as is indicated in Sidebar 10, Too Informal? Considering Appropriate Tone in Emails. When we encounter these sorts of situations, it is worth opening a one-on-one conversation with the student (orally or in writing) by noting our surprise at the student's behavior and asking questions about their intentions and assumptions.

There are some norms, however, with which we need to be flexible. For example, we may be accustomed to hugging students when we greet them after we have not seen them for a while or when congratulating them at graduation or another event. But some international students (and many domestic students, too, by the way) find this level of physical contact uncomfortable and would prefer to offer a handshake or even bump elbows instead. Another place for flexibility is in our approach to participation and collaboration: Knowing that many students come from less individualistic academic cultures, we can invite and even encourage students to work together during and outside of class. We can also broaden our conception of what "counts" as participation to include group work, deep listening, and other behaviors, as we touched on earlier. Chapters 3 and 4 offer additional pedagogical strategies that are inclusive of a range of academic cultural backgrounds and learning preferences.

Too Informal? Considering Appropriate Tone in Emails

At the end of the semester, a student from Kuwait wrote the following in an e-mail to her professor, requesting a grade change. If you received an e-mail like this from a student, how might you turn this into a "teachable moment" about appropriate tone in email communications?

";(there is no chance that u could change the grade ;(i really need it ;(.. And this is a second semester for me ;(and im international ! I had difficulties to understand in english ! And im doing my best ;(! .. Pleaseee is that possible we could make it to C ! I can't get into other class if you don't change it. I hope you could understand my situation."

Promote Student Interaction During and Outside of Class

As we touched on earlier, the interactions students have in our classes can help facilitate both academic learning and adjustment to U.S. academic culture. Yet interaction does not always happen automatically (Chen & Yeung, 2019). Large-group discussions can be culturally and linguistically challenging for international students. There are a number of other strategies and activities we can use in class to "ease the way" into large discussions and deepen students' relationships with their peers.

Here are some of our favorite activities for promoting interactions:

- **Think-pair-share (TPS).** In a TPS activity, students first reflect individually (often in writing) on a given question or concept. They then form pairs or small groups to share initial reflections. Finally, the whole class comes together to share highlights. One advantage of this activity over traditional discussion is that it provides opportunities for processing time, which is particularly helpful for students who feel less confident speaking in class. (See Chapter 3 for additional information about TPS.)

- **Global perspectives.** After considering an issue, event, or phenomenon from a U.S. perspective, we pause to invite students to bring in more global examples or points of view. We extend this invitation to everyone, recognizing that there may be domestic students in our classes who have lived abroad or follow international news. However, we find that international students are particularly appreciative of the opportunity to contribute in this way. They may share insights on policy (e.g., education, economics, health care) informed by other cultural perspectives or offer a case study (e.g., of social reform, community organizing, or other collective problem-solving). Here are two quick notes about inclusion with this type of activity: First, we try to give students advance notice so they have time to think about what they might share, rather than putting them "on the spot" (see Chapter 5 for more on this). Second, we avoid positioning a student as an "expert" or "representative voice" from their country, culture, or community. (For more examples of how we can make space for global and cross-cultural perspectives in our classes, see later in this chapter and more in Chapter 5.)

- **Just-in-time teaching.** One effective strategy for preparing students for class discussions is to have them post one or more questions or comments on an online discussion board (or send them via email) before class. We can then center part of the class lecture or discussion around those questions and comments. Once again, international students appreciate the opportunity for processing time, and it is gratifying for them when we take up a point or question they have raised during the class session. (We should be explicit with students about whether we will be linking questions and comments to specific students. Where possible, we try to make this the student's choice.)

- **Jigsaw reading.** With this activity, students select (or are assigned) a reading from a set of three or more (Readings A, B, C, etc.) to focus on for homework. As they read, their goal is to prepare to share highlights from their reading in the next class session. During class, students are first grouped with others who read the same reading (i.e., students who read A, students who read B, etc.) to compare notes and comments. Students are then placed in groups with classmates who read different pieces (e.g., one who read A, one who read B, one who read C, etc.) to share.

Again, we want to note two things before moving on. First, difficult situations sometimes emerge during class interactions, and our colleagues often ask us about how to respond in a way that is culturally inclusive. See Sidebar 08 for some common situations and options for addressing them. Second, when there is limited time for interaction during class, we can promote interaction outside of class by encouraging reading buddies or study groups, offering opportunities for students to collaborate on particular assignments, and publicizing (or even requiring) cocurricular and extracurricular events. See Chapter 5 for examples of how to encourage these interactions.

Promoting Cultural Inclusion in Course Content and Design

This chapter has focused primarily on academic culture and cultural adjustment as it relates to classroom instruction. However, we can also take cultural inclusion into account as we design and revise our courses. Research has found that students from underrepresented or marginalized groups—including international students—feel a greater sense of belonging at our institutions when they see a diverse range of backgrounds and perspectives represented in course materials and invited through assignment prompts (e.g., Arday et al., 2021; Sawir, 2013). Instructors across disciplines can widen this representation by considering questions such as these:

- How can I include more voices and perspectives in my course readings and media?

- How can I broaden the geographic and political contexts that are represented and/or invite students to link course learning to global contexts?

- If and when I reference popular culture (e.g., entertainment media, social media), how can I ensure that students who tend to engage with other media have the background information necessary to understand the reference?

- How might I welcome languages other than English into course lecture, assignments, and discussion (e.g., by inviting students to cite secondary sources written in other languages, perhaps with a brief explanatory footnote)?

Examples of how instructors in a variety of disciplines have answered these questions can be found in the remainder of this chapter, as well as in Chapter 5.

Recognizing Cultural Background Knowledge

Many instructors use references to popular culture (e.g., film, TV, music, sports, social media) to help students connect with course materials and concepts. However, these references can have the opposite effect for international students, who may not "get" the reference (see Sidebar 11, Examples of Cultural References).

This does not mean that we need to avoid all cultural references. Rather, we can ensure that all students understand those references by

- providing a bit of background on the source (e.g., "This clip is from a popular U.S. animated series for adults called *The Simpsons*. This show often references social and political issues in a satirical way.");

11

Examples of Cultural References

A. A Korean student in a sociology course was expected to know the "basics" of the U.S. legal system. His instructor encouraged students to think back to courtroom dramas on television, but this was not helpful to him, because such shows were not common on Korean TV.

B. A Chinese student found it frustrating that the readings and discussion in an art history class often referenced Biblical stories.

C. A Slovakian student in a political science class often felt left out when her professor told jokes that relied on knowledge of political parties in the United States.

D. A Japanese student in a gender studies course was told to write a letter to a parent or other family member explaining what he had learned in the class. He wrote in a formal style, as this is what is expected in his culture, but was graded down for not using an "authentic" voice.

- making media links available to students—ideally even before class—so they can explore and learn more on their own;

- directing students to reputable online or print sources where they can learn more about the particular media we are discussing; and

- giving students more options in their assignments (e.g., for the final example in Sidebar 11, the student could have been asked to write to someone using an informal tone).

Drawing on Students' Cultural and Global Knowledge

In almost any discipline, there are opportunities to draw on international students' cultural backgrounds and global perspectives to deepen learning for everyone. Here are examples of questions we might ask in different disciplines to invite these contributions in class discussion and student work:

- **Philosophy.** What are some of the contributions and critiques from scholars outside "Western" or Euro-centric traditions?

- **English literature.** What contributions have been made by writers using varieties of English other than U.S. and British? (Examples include Chinua Achebe, Arundhati Roy, and Salman Rushdie).

- **History, sociology, or political science.** How might our course concepts and theories be applied to case studies from outside the United States? How might immigrants and expatriates view these issues differently from citizens born in the country? (For example, students could compare the "American dream" to the "European dream"; e.g., Rifkin, 2013.)

- **STEM (science, technology, engineering, math).** How do the politics of academia impact what gets researched and who gets published? (This can include funding and technology, language priorities, access to technology and other resources, and systemic racism or other forms of oppression.) What issues might scientists in the United States overlook?

Building All Students' Intercultural Competence

A final reminder we wish to include is that the goal of cultural inclusion is to not only support the adjustment of international students but also help all students to engage across cultural differences. In fact, many colleges and universities include intercultural competence or global citizenship as a key component of their mission statements and learning outcomes (Aktas et al., 2017; Green, 2012). Some strategies that have been shown to build this skill set include the following:

- Invite students to respond to scenarios in which cultural differences play a role—perhaps even incorporating material from this chapter!

- Create classroom norms and structures that invite deep, empathic listening (see Chapter 3 for more on this strategy).

- Provide opportunities for students to facilitate discussions or present new materials so they have practice navigating power dynamics in classroom interactions.

Many of the strategies and activities that we will discuss in Chapter 3 can also help you build intercultural competence through student-to-student interaction.

Conclusion: Toward Cultural and Linguistic Inclusion for All

This chapter has highlighted the distinguishing features of the U.S. academic culture in higher education, including how these cultural features play out as international students transition into U.S. institutions. We hope the strategies, activities, and resources provided help build instructors' confidence and competence in working with students who have less experience with U.S. academic culture. As is the case with much of our pedagogical guidance, what works well with international students often works well with other groups, too. After all, U.S. academic culture is a strange place for many students, particularly those from underrepresented backgrounds. We hope the information in this chapter helps instructors promote cultural adjustment for all of their students.

The next chapter looks at language development as another factor that can have a major impact on the experiences of international students in U.S. higher education. Chapter 3 includes guidance on how to make our courses more linguistically accessible and inclusive. Before moving on, however, it is useful to consider how culture and language intersect. As was discussed throughout this chapter, cultural background knowledge is a central factor in students' comprehension of lectures and assigned readings. Thus, if international students are struggling with course materials, there may be both cultural and linguistic factors at play. The same is true when it comes to expectations for classroom behaviors (e.g., contributing to class discussion), teacher-student interactions, and assignments. We hope you will keep in mind the insights about cultural adjustment from this chapter as you learn more about language support in Chapter 3.

CHAPTER 3

Supporting Language Development With Linguistically Inclusive Pedagogy

This chapter aims to increase instructors' understanding of pedagogical effectiveness for working with international students for whom English is an additional language. We first explore what it means to know another language and the variables that influence an individual's level of attainment. Then, we highlight three basic second language acquisition (SLA) principles—scaffolding, interaction, and noticing—and present instructional practices informed by these principles, which can make our instruction more inclusive of international students from a variety of language backgrounds. In these ways, we help instructors move toward more linguistically inclusive pedagogy that can support international students' ongoing language and literacy development, as well as their learning of academic content.

A linguistically inclusive approach is one that sees language difference as an asset, rather than a problem. Moreover, it urges us to see ourselves as language teachers, because academic language, modes of inquiry and argumentation, and writing and literacy conventions are all part of the content students are learning in our courses (e.g., Blok et al., 2020; Haan & Gallagher, 2022; Gallagher & Haan, 2018; Tomaš & Shapiro, 2021). This shift in our understanding of language in the classroom can be quite transformative for instructors, as indicated by the quotations in Sidebar 12, Instructor Perspectives.

What Does It Mean to Know an Additional Language?

Attaining proficiency in an additional language is a complex process involving the development of

> **Instructor Perspectives**
>
> "I used to get really worked up about my international students' 'atrocious' grammar usage in their papers. After taking a workshop on working with international students, I realized that expecting my students to write at the same level as native speakers is simply not realistic. This realization helped me . . . focus instead on their ideas, logic, and organization."
> —*Instructor in nutrition*
>
> "I found my international students have some of the best theoretical grasp of the material, even if their English writing skills still needed work."
> —*Instructor in communication*

language skills (reading, writing, listening, speaking) and subskills (grammar, vocabulary, pronunciation). It involves not only accuracy but also fluency and appropriateness: A language user whose speech or writing is "error free" may not be viewed as proficient if the language seems choppy, stilted, or ill-suited to the situation at hand.

Proficiency is also defined by the needs of the language user. For example, a shopkeeper working in a foreign country may be able to communicate proficiently as long as they have conversational language skills (e.g., to interact comfortably with customers) as well as some specialized language for business purpose (e.g., financial vocabulary, language for publicity and advertising). On the other hand, an engineer working for an international company may primarily need to know how to function within a specific workplace domain rather than attaining a high level of general communication proficiency. A student planning to study at a U.S. college or university, in further contrast, needs a considerably broader repertoire of linguistic and academic skills that will allow them to engage with course content and to participate in the academic community.

Clearly, all of these learners need to know the target language, although *what* they need to know differs. All of these learners can be successful in using the language, even if they never sound "native-like." This is an important consideration regarding the international students in our classes. One of our goals in this chapter is to help instructors set and support realistic expectations by considering what international students need most to succeed at U.S. colleges and universities. (See Sidebar 13, Reflection Questions About Language Learning.)

> **13**
>
> **Reflection Questions About Language Learning**
>
> A. What kinds of experiences have you had with studying additional languages?
>
> B. Do you consider yourself a "good" language learner? Why or why not?
>
> C. What helped—and what hindered—your development of proficiency in another language?
>
> D. Have you ever felt excluded or judged because of your language use?
>
> E. Have you ever felt that you needed to change the way you speak or write in order to be successful in school?

What Do Test Scores Tell Us About Students' English Proficiency?

Most institutions of higher education require or encourage international students to submit some kind of test score noting their English language proficiency. The two most common test scores used by U.S. colleges and universities are the Test of English as a Foreign Language (TOEFL) and the International English Language Testing System (IELTS), but other tests, such as the Duolingo English Test (DET), have become increasingly common in recent years. (See Appendix G for more information on these and other commonly used English language tests.)

Studies have found that there is some correlation between these tests and students' academic performance in higher education (e.g., Avdi, 2011; Cho & Bridgeman, 2012), although research is inconclusive about whether these tests actually provide enough information to guide institutional decision-making around admissions and academic support (e.g., Jenkins & Leung, 2019; Pearson, 2021). And of course, there are logistical concerns about the potential stress students face in preparing and paying for these expensive exams. Because of these concerns, we advise instructors to see English test scores as one of many indicators of what students know and can do with English. Another reason for this caution is that there are a variety of factors that can influence students' experiences with language learning, as we discuss in the next section.

Factors in Language Acquisition

How long does it take to acquire an additional language? What determines success in learning a language? Why might the English language proficiency of international students vary widely? These questions have been the focus of decades of applied linguistics research. As with most complex processes, success in learning a language is determined by the interplay of many factors. The scope of this chapter does not allow for an in-depth examination of all known variables; instead, we will briefly describe those factors that have been consistently identified as most important in determining language learning outcomes and that might shed light on the experiences, strengths, and needs of international students for whom English is an additional language.

Environmental Factors

The nature of instruction and the amount of exposure to the language are important environmental factors in language learning. Some international students may say they started learning English in elementary school, but they still have not attained an advanced level of fluency. This is because the quality of English instruction varies widely; some students may have learned English grammar in large classes but never had the opportunity to practice speaking and writing, for example. Moreover, many students have never studied academic subjects in English and therefore struggle to learn the disciplinary language (see Sidebar 14, Student Perspectives on Using English as an Additional Language).

First or home language (L1) also plays a role in learning an additional language. Students from language backgrounds similar to the target language are better positioned to master that new language than students who come from language backgrounds that are considerably different (Jarvis & Pavlenko, 2008). Consider, for example, Arabic students learning English—they not only have to master a new alphabet but also have to learn to write from left to right! Chinese or Thai students, whose first languages are tonal, have to learn to use tone for different purposes in English, such as to signal a question versus a statement. Mastering such major linguistic differences takes a long time for users of languages that are considerably distinct from English.

> **14**
>
> **Student Perspectives on Using English as an Additional Language**
>
> "There was definitely a great shock after coming here because my English has always been the best among my peers, but here I was like only a decent writer among Americans."
> —*Student from China*
>
> "I am often the only nonnative English speaker in class. It always takes a little bit of (actually a lot of) courage to speak up on the first day of classes because I know that I speak English differently from most of my peers and I am afraid that my classmates would judge me. . . . All these thoughts linger in my mind."
> —*Student from Japan*

Psychological Factors

Although psychological influences on language learning are difficult to investigate, most existing literature shows that successful language learners tend to have an optimal level of anxiety (e.g., Dörnyei, 2005; Oxford, 1999). Learners who feel overly anxious about using the target language are less likely to progress as effectively with language learning. Successful language learners also typically possess a high level of self-confidence that makes them willing to communicate and take risks; hence, extroverts are said to be better language learners, at least when it comes to speaking fluently. On the other hand, introverts are often better at language learning tasks that require attention to accuracy (Dewaele & Furnham, 1999; Dörnyei, 2005). A high tolerance for ambiguity is also beneficial in language learning, as learners must be able to deal with the frustration that accompanies gaps in comprehension, exceptions to grammatical rules, cultural miscommunications, and other challenges (Ehrman, 1999).

Two additional psychosocial factors have been discussed frequently in the literature: motivation and strategy use. There are two main types of motivation in learning an additional language: instrumental motivation (learning language for personal gain) and integrative motivation (learning language in order to engage with a particular group). Both types of motivation are believed to play a positive role in language learning success (Dörnyei, 1990). Motivation is not "fixed," however: Research shows that instructors can have a major effect on language learners' motivation through high-impact instructional strategies (e.g., Guilloteaux & Dörnyei, 2008) and promotion of a growth mindset (Ng, 2018; Yeager & Dweck, 2020).

Finally, successful language learners need to develop a repertoire of learning strategies (Oxford, 2017), including metacognitive skills that promote awareness of their own thinking and learning. Successful language learners are also able to employ a range of academic strategies (e.g., note-taking, summarizing and synthesizing information) and socio-affective strategies (e.g., interacting with peers) to help them cope with linguistic challenges (O'Malley & Chamot, 1990). In fact, we have found that international students can be helpful in sharing these strategies with domestic students who are in the process of learning additional languages or preparing to study abroad.

Sociocultural Factors

A final set of factors has to do with the social and cultural contexts in which students are learning English, as well as what type of English they have learned. Many international students come to us from countries that were former British colonies (e.g., India, Kenya, Singapore) and therefore may have learned a dialect of English different from what is considered "standardized" in the United States. Instructors unfamiliar with World Englishes may count something as an error that is in fact "correct" according to other standards (e.g., "to take a decision" is a commonly used construction in British and Indian Englishes, whereas U.S. English uses "to make a decision"). The academic cultures in which students have learned English (or *learnt* in the British English variety) also play a role: We may have students whose studies of English took place almost entirely via reading and writing and who struggle mightily with listening and speaking.

Sociocultural factors and past educational experiences also shape students' understandings of academic writing. As we explored in Chapter 2, students who have had less practice writing in the styles most common at U.S. academic institutions—styles that prioritize argumentation, efficiency, and linearity—may produce writing that is perceived by U.S.-educated instructors as unclear or indirect. The difference between the two is less about language and more about culturally informed rhetorical expectations (Connor, 1996; Kubota & Lehner, 2004).

Identity, Power, and Privilege

It is also important to notice that students' social identities, as well as their racial, economic, and other privileges (or lack thereof), have a significant impact on their language learning trajectories (Darvin & Norton, 2021). In many countries, opportunities for high-quality English instruction are only available to students from wealthier backgrounds. Moreover, research has found that linguistic racism—that is, the disparate treatment of certain groups of language users based on systemic racism—is prevalent in higher education, including against international students (e.g., Dovchin, 2020). For example, students who are white (or who can "pass" as white) are often assumed to speak English as their first language, based solely on their physical appearance (Amin, 1997).

One key takeaway from this line of research is that students' engagement in language learning is shaped by their identities, assets, and lived experiences. This is why a number of scholars have suggested a shift in focus from *motivation*, which is often thought of as an individual, psychological phenomenon, to *investment*, which is both social and structural. This shift invites us to consider questions such as the following: What are students able to invest (intellectually, socially, emotionally, logistically) in language learning, and how do differences in privilege impact how those investments are perceived? How can instructors and administrators recognize and reward student investment? (See Darvin, 2020, for more on this topic.) The answers to these questions, in turn, help us strategize what we teach and how.

Implications for Instructors

Clearly, many of the factors that impact language development are out of the instructor's control. However, this information is useful to keep in mind, for several reasons. First, as we alluded to earlier, it is normal to see a range of English language abilities among international students, and this variation is not necessarily the result of factors over which students have control. Because there are so many factors that influence students' language learning trajectories, we cannot assume that a student who seems more confident with English is more hardworking, capable, or intelligent than any other student.

There are ethical implications for this as well: Because "native-like" proficiency is unlikely (and unnecessary) for most learners of English as an additional language (e.g., Birdsong, 2006), we as instructors must evaluate students fairly on the content and clarity of their work, rather than making the native speaker the "gold standard" (e.g., Matsuda et al., 2003; more on this in Chapter 4 as well). Just as we expect a variety of spoken accents in our classrooms, because our students often come from many regions and countries, we should expect to see "written accents" in texts produced by multilingual writers (e.g., Harris & Silva, 1993; Choi, 2016). In this way, we can work against "native-speakerism," which is prevalent in higher education and harmful to both students and instructors who use global varieties of English that are prevalent outside the United States (e.g., Choi, 2016).

An understanding of these factors also helps us think about what we as instructors can do to increase access for international students who are also multilingual. For example, recognizing that anxiety is a major factor in language learning (and in academic performance overall), we can use strategies presented later in this chapter and elsewhere in the book that provide students with the support and clarity they need to manage that anxiety. We can also help students figure out what aspects are within their control (such as use of learning strategies) and outside their control (such as the "native-ness" of their speech and writing) so they can experience greater ownership of their language learning, both inside and outside the classroom. Finally, reminding international students of the great value in being multilingual can go a long way in fostering their confidence and a growth mindset so they are less focused on perceived linguistic and cultural "deficiencies."

Awareness of the factors discussed earlier provides insight into how we can treat multilingualism as an asset. As we will continue discussing in Chapters 4 and 5, there are a number of ways we can indicate to students that we see being multilingual (and multidialectal) as a resource instead of a deficit. We may, for example, include readings or media that incorporate multiple varieties of English, such as TED Talks from users of different World Englishes. We can also welcome the use of secondary sources in languages other than English and invite students to use a broader range of languages and dialects in some of their oral or written work, where appropriate. Options like these not only increase confidence for multilingual students but also help increase *everyone's* awareness of and appreciation for linguistic diversity (e.g., Losey & Shuck, 2021; Shapiro, 2022).

Principles for Linguistically Inclusive Instruction

While there is a great deal of research on how instructors can best support students who are still in the process of language development, we have chosen to focus on three core SLA principles in this chapter: (i) scaffolding, (ii) interaction, and (iii) noticing. In this section, we present each principle and outline corresponding instructional strategies, many of which will be discussed more thoroughly later in the chapter. (See also Sidebar 15, Reflection Questions About Teaching New Terms and Concepts.)

Scaffolding

The concept of scaffolding first emerged out of research in first language acquisition, in which it was observed that adults tend to adapt their ways of speaking to facilitate language development in children (e.g., Bruner, 1985). Since then, the term has been applied to a variety of other learning situations and is now used in SLA (and in education more broadly) to describe the various ways that teachers adapt their instruction to support students in reaching high levels of achievement. Instructors can provide scaffolding in a number of ways, such as paying attention to their own speech (e.g., pacing, emphasis, word choice, etc.); using visuals and other media in a lecture; and teaching explicit strategies for effective reading, writing, or other academic tasks (see also Blok et al., 2020; Jiang, 2012; Walqui, 2006).

Interaction

While scaffolding is often focused on the input provided by instructors (and sometimes peers), interaction has to do with the other end of the instructional process: output (Swain, 1985; Hall & Verplaetse, 2000). Tasks that require interaction among students tend to promote language development and content learning; they can include pair and small-group discussion, as well as activities such as peer review, group work, or collaborative projects. One of the reasons interaction is so important is that it gives students the opportunity to receive feedback on whether they are communicating effectively, which builds their confidence for future interactions (Loewen & Sato, 2018; Long, 1983; Pica et al., 1996). Interaction can also happen virtually through online discussion, shared documents, and other collaboration tools.

Noticing

The last SLA principle that can help guide instruction for international students is noticing. The original noticing hypothesis (Schmidt, 1990) states that conscious attention to linguistic input is a prerequisite for adult language learning. Learners who are attuned to patterns in a language will likely acquire that language more quickly. Instructors can incorporate this principle by highlighting discipline-specific vocabulary, writing conventions, and other particularities of their field. Of course, doing so requires that instructors develop an awareness of how language is used in their discipline and recognize that they may have "expert blind spots" about what may be unfamiliar to students (Nathan & Petrosino, 2003).

> **15**
>
> **Reflection Questions About Teaching New Terms and Concepts**
>
> 1. What are some of the discipline-specific terms or concepts that students might not know prior to taking your class?
>
> 2. What has helped you learn new terms or concepts (or vocabulary in another language)?
>
> 3. How might you create opportunities for your students to encounter key vocabulary in your classes more frequently so they can retain the vocabulary?
>
> 4. How might you apply the SLA principles (scaffolding, interaction, noticing) to make these terms more comprehensible to students (e.g., during class lecture)?

Pedagogical Applications for Scaffolding, Interaction, and Noticing

In the remainder of this chapter, we provide a number of strategies and activities instructors can use for effective classroom instruction, which are underwritten by these principles of scaffolding, interaction, and noticing. We have organized this section according to the following components of instruction: assigned readings and media, in-class lecture, and group discussion. Near the end of the chapter, we provide additional strategies for promoting lifelong language learning. In Chapter 4, we will return to some of these concepts to consider ways to design and scaffold assignments and other forms of assessment.

One of the strategies we will discuss is to provide tools such as graphic organizers to help students keep track of key information as they read, listen, discuss, and so on. Figure 3.1 is a sample graphic organizer that you might even want to use as you engage with the material we present in this chapter! A downloadable version of this organizer is available on the companion website for this book (www.tesol.org/FISS).

Figure 3.1 *Sample Reading Guide (Graphic Organizer)*

SLA principles	Suggested ideas from text	Additional ideas I have
For course readings and media		
Scaffolding ➜		
Interaction ➜		
Noticing ➜		
For class lecture		
Scaffolding ➜		
Interaction ➜		
Noticing ➜		
For class discussion		
Scaffolding ➜		
Interaction ➜		
Noticing ➜		
For other aspects of pedagogy		
Scaffolding ➜		
Interaction ➜		
Noticing ➜		

Supporting Students' Engagement With Assigned Readings and Media

Academic reading tends to be a challenge for many international students (Andrade, 2006). Many instructors assign a large amount of reading for each class, and those readings often contain dense, discipline-specific language. Several strategies can be used to support students in reading effectively.

Providing Scaffolding for Course Readings and Media

Be intentional in selecting course readings. Many instructors do not take the time to calculate the total number of pages assigned to students or the time they expect students to spend completing the readings. By thinking carefully about how much time students should allot for reading, instructors can ensure that the workload for their class is reasonable.

Make expectations for reading explicit. There are many types of and purposes for course readings, and students are sometimes confused about the goals and expectations for the readings. Be transparent with students about why you have chosen each reading, how it contributes to their course learning, and what they should focus on as they read. Sometimes instructors simply expect that students will "skim" a reading, but students may think they are expected to read closely and make detailed annotations.

Activate students' background knowledge. Reading comprehension is greatly enhanced when students are able to relate what they are about to read to what they already know. Instructors can activate this prior knowledge by having students discuss and brainstorm, conduct internet searches, and preview a text together, making predictions and inferences. (*Note:* Many of the activities mentioned later in relation to class discussion also work well for this purpose.)

Identify resources with relevant background information. International students will appreciate knowing about websites, articles, books, and other resources that provide background information about the reading and help define key terms and concepts. Resources that are brief and less dense than the assigned reading are the most helpful. Cultural background information can also be particularly helpful for students who grew up outside the United States, as we discussed in Chapter 2.

Provide students with guiding questions or a task to complete as they read. We might provide a chart or an outline and ask students to fill in missing information.

16

Resource for Guided Reading

A guided reading resource can be extremely helpful to students. As one example, we might ask students to engage in the following process before, during, and after reading. For a downloadable worksheet that students can use during this process, visit the companion website for this book (www. tesol.org/FISS).

Before

Preview and connect (identify purpose, genre, features, main topics, essential terminology, etc.)

Predict (set up for note-taking, using subheadings)

During

Reading log (includes three columns for note-taking: page/section; main idea, quote, or concept; and reaction or question)

After

Summarize (What are some main points, comments/connections, and questions?)

Reflect (How does this reading fit with the larger map of the course? What does it add? Does it challenge or deepen any earlier theories, arguments, or case studies?)

Takeaways

Key points, comments, questions (Students can bring these up in class discussions or written work.)

We can also use reading logs, in which students take note of salient points or quotes from the text, then write a comment or question in response. Visual and graphic organizers are useful for increasing students' comprehension of complex texts (Blok et al., 2020; Jiang, 2012) and preparing students to complete writing assignments based on content (Styati & Irawati, 2020). Requiring these tasks also helps the instructor hold students accountable for completing the reading. (See Figure 3.1 for a sample graphic organizer that can be used to facilitate *your* reading of this chapter; also see Sidebar 16, Resource for Guided Reading.)

Broaden the types of material assigned. Today's students have access to a great deal of high-quality multimedia materials online and via social media. We have found that there are often audio, video, or other multimedia resources that are just as effective as a traditional reading list—if not more so—at presenting academic content. Moreover, additional media often come with particular features that make the content more engaging and accessible. Podcasts and videos, for example, can be played back at a slower (or faster) speed and may come with transcripts or subtitles as well. Instructors can further scaffold multimedia through technologies such as Edpuzzle, which is a useful tool for flipped classrooms, which we discuss later this chapter. Instructors can use original videos or draw from YouTube, TED.com, and other sites, then punctuate the video with instructor-generated audio notes and questions that students engage with as they watch. Of course, students are excellent curators of new media for us as well. We often invite them to share links to relevant media with us and with each other!

Encouraging Interaction Around Course Readings and Media

When students have the opportunity to engage with each other around our course materials, this increases their comprehension, as well as their overall academic performance. Moreover, this builds their connections with one another, resulting in a greater sense of social integration and belonging. Here are some suggestions for promoting these interactions:

- **Prepare interactive tasks based on the readings.** Work assigned to accompany the readings can be used as the basis for in-class interaction. Students can rely on their written work (e.g., notes, charts, etc.) as a reference, which encourages a higher level of engagement during discussion and group work.

- **Use technological tools to encourage out-of-class interaction.** There are many apps, websites, and other technologies that allow students to annotate and discuss course materials. Some of our favorites include Hypothes.is, Jamboard, and Padlet. Group chat apps such as Discord and Slack can also be used for this purpose. In her course on public speaking, for example, Raichle (one of this book's authors) has students create short presentations that emulate best practices from a TED Talk of their choice that they share on Padlet for feedback. Zuzana, another author, has students cocreate websites in which they share course learning with a large audience. These kinds of technologies can also allow students to create coauthored resources, such as guidebooks or writing anthologies.

- **Create opportunities to practice critical response.** Students can learn to engage more critically with course readings through small-group discussion, peer review, debate, or role-play. These activities help students imagine or discover what a critic would say. (See Shapiro & Leopold, 2012, for more on how role-play can facilitate critical thinking.)

- **Consider assigning different readings to each group.** Rather than assigning multiple readings for everyone, we can divide the class into groups and ask each group to read a different text and prepare to share key points or reactions to that reading in a small group with students who were assigned a different text. This is sometimes called "jigsaw reading" because each student has a piece that they put together to increase learning for the entire group. We can then come together as a large group to share what we have learned about all of the readings or media presented. (See Appendix A for more information on implementing jigsaw activities.)

Facilitating Noticing in Course Readings

Cultivate prereading skills. Encourage students to preview the text prior to reading, either alone or with peers. Draw their attention to what they might look for before they tackle the text, such as length, organization, headings, visuals, keywords, and guiding concepts. Invite students to predict what they will read in the text and craft questions they hope the author will answer, based on their preview of the text.

Model effective strategies to employ while reading the text. Students appreciate explicit discussion of strategies for reading, including what sequence they should read in (e.g., for a scientific journal article, it might be best to read the Discussion and Conclusion sections before reading the Methods and Findings sections so they understand the "So what?" of the study). We can model for students how to engage physically with the text (e.g., making notes in the margin, highlighting key points). It is also helpful to highlight some potentially detrimental reading habits that our students might have developed, such as looking up every unfamiliar vocabulary word (see Sidebar 17, Tips for Dealing With Difficult Reading Passages). We can also invite students to share their strategies with their classmates, which may include ideas we have not considered.

Cornell Notes is a reading sequence many of our students find helpful. The sequence begins with previewing and predicting, then concludes with summarizing key points from the reading. See Sidebar 16, Resource for Guided Reading, which is based on this sequence. For links to video tutorials and other resources related to the Cornell Notes sequence, visit the companion website for this book (www.tesol.org/FISS).

A more pared-down approach that one author, Shawna, uses frequently is what she calls 3-2-1 Reading. This approach, which is designed to help students read efficiently and effectively to prepare for class discussion, asks students to come away from the reading with

- 3 main points or concepts;
- 2 connections (to self, other texts, or the world); and
- 1 question or "muddy point" for clarification.

For a link to a handout that can be used to scaffold the 3-2-1 Reading approach, visit the companion website for this book (www.tesol.org/FISS). Zuzana uses a similar tool but also asks students to choose a phrase or quotation that caught their attention so they can engage with the text and also notice the author's linguistic choices.

Help students make use of course readings and media in their own work. As we will discuss further in Chapter 4, reading and writing are interconnected, and effective scaffolding, noticing, and interaction with one will feed into better outcomes for the others.

Supporting Students' Comprehension of Course Lectures

Despite numerous concerns about its pedagogical effectiveness, oral lecturing persists as the predominant mode of instruction in higher education worldwide (Bligh, 2000; Chaudhury, 2011). Delivering lectures is relatively convenient (especially for large classes) and allows the instructor to assume some level of control over the presentation of information. Lectures can be informative and compelling with an effective speaker, but they tend to keep students in a relatively passive role. Research suggests that international students often struggle in lecture-based classes (e.g., Andrade, 2006; Littlemore et al., 2011). This is in part because listening comprehension and note-taking can be difficult when working in an additional language—particularly when instructors speak quickly, use a high amount of colloquial language or discipline-specific vocabulary, or rely heavily on text rather than including visuals.

In fact, traditional oral lectures are demanding for most learners—including fluent English speakers—because attention and working memory are strained (Jeffries & Huggett, 2014). Brief lectures (i.e., 15–20 minutes) that include active-learning opportunities and peer interaction have been found to increase student comprehension and learning (Bligh, 2000; Cooper & Richards, 2016; Smith et al., 2009). For example, instructors may intersperse lectures with discussion prompts, application tasks, and other activities to keep students engaged and to gather feedback on student learning (more on this in Chapter 4). Next, we discuss strategies that we can use to increase the comprehensibility and effectiveness of our lectures for all students.

Scaffolding the Lecture

Make goals and expectations explicit. Students learn much more from lectures when they have a clear sense of purpose. Some of the questions we can answer for students in the first week—and on a regular basis—include the following:

- How do the assigned readings and media relate to the lecture? Do they address the same information, just in different formats, or do they complement each other in different ways?

- How much detail are students expected to retain from lectures? How will they know whether they have gained what they need?

- What should students do if they are having trouble comprehending the lecture?

Activate students' background knowledge and prior learning. It is a worthwhile use of class time to review key concepts or skills from the previous class and to field questions based on assignments and readings. This not only helps students connect old learning to new learning but also allows us to make clarifications that may increase their comprehension of new material. Moreover, when introducing new topics, it is helpful to build on what students already know. Prelistening activities can help students "warm up" to the key topics and questions and begin to activate their prior knowledge about the lecture topic. (See Sidebar 18, Activating Background Knowledge: Case Study of a Human Anatomy Course, for an example.) Here are a couple of strategies:

- Ask students to free-write or brainstorm orally some thoughts related to the content of the lecture, possibly in pairs or small groups. (E.g., "Before we talk about this text, let's predict what concerns might have been raised about it at the time it was published.")

- Provide a task students can engage in before the lecture. For example, students might be asked to group key scientific terms into categories, give real-world examples to match sociological theories, or identify passages in a literary text that address particular themes.

Use predictable sequencing. International students appreciate having consistent learning sequences in our classes, including for our lectures. Using similar structures for lectures can provide some consistency that helps lower anxiety and increase engagement and comprehension. For example, it is helpful to begin a lecture with an outline and a list of learning objectives, including sharing how the new material fits with what students learned in the previous class. As noted earlier, using smaller, 15- to 20-minute "chunks" is recommended, with short interactive activities in between (e.g., a simple "turn-and-talk" to check in with a peer about a concept or reflection question). It is helpful to conclude each lecture with an opportunity to summarize and make connections to core concepts and essential questions.

Pay attention to the rate and quality of speech. It is helpful to many students when we speak in a way that is relaxed, rather than hurried, and take time to pause between important points or concepts. This gives slower processers time to follow what we are saying. When using slides, it is effective to wait a few seconds before moving to the next slide. Some instructors also allow students to audio-record the lecture so they can listen again after class. For courses taught online, there may be additional options such as live captioning or transcripts that can aid student comprehension. It is also helpful to pay careful attention to our use of pop culture references, as we discussed in Chapter 2. These can include metaphors that require specific cultural knowledge, such as the baseball analogy "out in left field" or the football metaphor "the whole nine yards."

Repeat, or have students restate, important information. Repetition is of tremendous help to international students, but it can be quite useful to others as well who might be struggling with comprehension for a variety of reasons (learning differences, less experience with the topic, etc.). It is extremely helpful to students when we repeat key words and ideas throughout the lecture. For those "big ideas" that we want students to take away, we should aim to repeat them at least three times during the lesson by "recycling" the information back into the presentation on intermittent review slides or jotting key points on the board and referring to them multiple times. Providing opportunities for students to paraphrase key points is another way to review the material and to solidify student understanding (see the next section for more on this strategy).

Provide a graphic organizer. Graphic organizers include flowcharts, grids, incomplete outlines, clusters, or other visual representations of information. As students listen to the lecture, they can complete the graphic organizer. This can also be an opportunity for peer-to-peer interaction, as discussed in the next section. (As a reminder, Figure 3.1 is a sample graphic organizer related to the content of this chapter.)

Supplement lectures with visual support. Visual support can include diagrams, charts, images, and other media (e.g., video and film). Visuals provide additional nonlinguistic information to activate students' existing background knowledge of a topic and illustrate abstract or unfamiliar concepts. At the very least, we should use presentation slides or the board to reinforce main points and key words, rather than simply presenting information orally. One reason for this is that students who are unfamiliar with particular words may be able to look for them in a bilingual dictionary if they see them in writing.

Encouraging Interaction During the Lecture

Provide opportunities for students to engage actively with the material. As mentioned earlier, it is useful to organize lectures into 15- to 20-minute chunks, with meaningful interactive tasks in between. Well-designed interactive tasks not only promote active learning but also serve as a comprehension check, providing instructors with additional feedback about student learning. Here are several examples to consider:

- **Review questions.** Have students work collaboratively to respond to prompts about the recently presented material. After the allotted time, we can call on students at random to share their responses. This can also be done as a think-pair-share (see the next suggestion). Where possible, we should craft these questions to reflect what students might see on a quiz or exam.

- **Think-Pair-Share.** Give students time to think and perhaps jot down a few ideas individually in response to a prompt. Then, have them continue the discussion in pairs, followed by a debrief with another pair or with the larger group (see Sidebar 19, Instructions for Think-Pair-Share).

- **Group problem-solving.** Design an activity that allows students to apply the theory or content to a scenario they might encounter outside of class. This might be a case study to reflect on, a quantitative problem to solve, or a report or proposal to evaluate. Students can share their responses with the class verbally or present them on the board.

- **Peer-to-peer instruction.** It is helpful to stop at various points during the lecture to let students compare notes or complete graphic organizers. All students will benefit from seeing how their peers organize and understand information. International students may appreciate the opportunity to see their domestic peers' note-taking strategies, including English abbreviations and shorthand.

Encourage out-of-class study buddies or groups. Provide time early in the semester for students to get to know one another so they can exchange contact information. Students can be encouraged to offer accountability and feedback on papers, projects, and other assignments. Many instructors also use online spaces (e.g., Blackboard, Canvas by Instructure, Google Classroom, Slack Channels) to promote student-student interactions outside of class.

There are a number of other ways to encourage students' interaction with us and each other during and after the lecture. One strategy is to use frequent comprehension checks, which are short tasks or prompts that give us immediate feedback on student learning (see Sidebar 20, Tips for Using Comprehension Checks). These checks not only reinforce learning but also become a means of formative assessment for us as instructors (more on this in Chapter 4). International students tend to be particularly appreciative of the opportunity to have information recycled and to assess their own understanding. (*Note:* Most instructors find that it works best to plan these tasks or questions ahead of time to ensure they are clear and well timed.)

One of the simplest activities is to ask students to pair up and summarize a portion of the lecture (or other media) that has just been presented. Or we can ask questions that students respond to through choral response—for example, asking a subset of students (e.g., "just those in the back row") to respond from time to time. We can also invite kinesthetic responses, using what Staley (2003) calls "visible quizzes."

19

Instructions for Think-Pair-Share

- Choose a relatively complex prompt (or series of questions) that students will benefit from processing both alone and in groups. Before initiating the "think" portion, provide an overview of the activity sequence. First, go over the instructions and prompt(s), perhaps doing a quick comprehension check (see Sidebar 20, Tips for Using Comprehension Checks) to make sure students all know what is expected.

- For the "think" portion, give students options of writing in any language, and make sure they know that the purpose of the writing is simply to facilitate their own reflection.

- During the "pair" phase, which can also be done in small groups, it can be helpful to walk around and listen to students' ideas. This will help you identify the themes and decide which pairs you might call on if no one volunteers. Students are more likely to ask clarifying questions as well if they see the instructor nearby. If you notice U.S. students dominating exchanges that include international students, sit with that pair or group for a bit to encourage a more proportional discussion.

- For the whole-class "share" phase, you can "cold call" students without too much concern about scaring them because they have been "warmed up." At this point, you can foster contributions from international students by calling on those pairs and the international students by name.

Students can raise hands, show fingers, or stand or sit to demonstrate true or false and agree or disagree. For multiple-choice questions, we can hand out color-coded or numbered cards that map to different answers. These cards can also be used for students' self-assessment (e.g., "Show green if you're ready to move on or yellow if you'd like us to practice this skill a bit more."). This technique allows the instructor to see which individuals may need more review, in addition to getting an overall assessment of the group's learning.

Many instructors incorporate technological tools to provide immediate feedback about student learning, such as survey tools (e.g., Poll Everywhere) and online quiz applications (e.g., Kahoot!) that students can use on their phones or laptops. These tools can help us identify points that need further clarification and are also a great way to get a sense of group preferences in classes where students may be reluctant to raise hands. Instructors teaching remotely may have access to this survey technology as part of their meeting technology (e.g., Google Meet, Zoom). Questions can target content, such as this example from an introduction to linguistics course: "In the following sentence, what is the grammatical function of the underlined phrase?" Or these questions can be used so students can self-assess for understanding, similar to the physical and visual responses noted in Sidebar 20.

20

Tips for Using Comprehension Checks

- Ask meaningful questions that require students to provide some content as a way of demonstrating understanding (e.g., "What are the first three steps in this process?" or "How many X do we need to complete this activity?"). These questions are likely to provide more useful information than prompts such as "Do you understand?" or "Do you have any questions?"

- Provide ample wait time after you ask a question. Give students 5–10 seconds (or longer). The silence may feel awkward, but students need time to process the question and think of the response.

- Invite physical or visual responses, such as "Give me a thumbs-up/down/sideways" or "Using a scale of 1 (not understanding at all) to 5 (complete understanding), hold up fingers to indicate how well you understand this concept/process."

Facilitating Noticing in a Lecture

Highlight and reinforce key terms and concepts. Students find it incredibly helpful to have lists of key vocabulary to inform their lecture listening (and their engagement with course materials, as discussed earlier). We can provide a list ahead of time or display keywords on the board or screen during the lecture or discussion. It is also useful to refer back to these terms as much as possible, perhaps using highlighting, bold text, or underlining. For terms that are difficult to pronounce, practicing together can build everyone's confidence. When appropriate, use synonyms, mnemonics, or other techniques to help students remember key terms. Instructors can also provide opportunities for students to use the terms in class activities and assignments (e.g., oral summary, response paper, student-generated test questions).

Utilize key phrases (i.e., verbal signposts) to focus student attention. International students—all students, in fact—benefit from hearing verbal cues that highlight what is important (e.g., "The most important point to take away from this section is ..."), signify order or indicate a series (e.g., *first, second, next, finally*), and introduce contradictions or controversies (e.g., *on the other hand, in contrast, unlike her colleagues*). When these signposts are used consistently, students will be primed to recognize them in the lecture.

Cultivate effective listening strategies. Create tasks that require students to pay attention and practice listening skills such as predicting, summarizing, elaborating, and organizing information. For example, we might ask students to

- anticipate a topic based on a hook (e.g., quote, picture, introduction to lecture);
- write two main points from the lecture to share with a peer; or
- craft questions for discussion or clarification as they listen. (The 3-2-1 Reading approach discussed earlier is also useful for this purpose.)

In particular, we find students appreciate opportunities to make connections to self, other texts, and the world.

Remind students of resources that can aid their listening. Students sometimes forget about some of the built-in features that can aid their comprehension. We may provide slides or handouts that students can use to take notes as they follow along with the lecture. When we show media clips to students, we can enable subtitles or captioning, as these can help with comprehension. (Many websites, such as YouTube, now enable this feature for all available content. The technology is not perfect, but it often helps!) Auto-captioning can be a resource for online courses, too, helping to ensure that all aspects of the course are more accessible for everyone. As noted earlier, for students who continue to struggle with live, face-to-face lectures, we may give them the option of audio-recording the lecture on their cell phones—and perhaps even make those recordings available to others in the class.

Before moving on, we wish to remind readers that many of the suggestions in this section might also be helpful for students who have difficulties with auditory processing, attention, and other issues, regardless of their language background. This illustrates, once again, that we can expand access for a variety of students as we make adaptations with the particular needs of international students in mind, thus making our courses more inclusive and equitable for everyone. One final option we want to mention is using a "flipped classroom" model, in which students engage with the lecture material before class and class time is used to review, clarify, and apply core concepts. (See Sidebar 21, The Flipped Classroom.)

Supporting Class Discussion

Class discussion can be another major challenge for international students (Andrade, 2006; Hsu & Huang, 2017; Morita, 2004). Students may be hesitant

---

The Flipped Classroom 21

In recent years, many instructors in higher education have experimented with "flipping" classroom instruction. This means that much of their course content is provided outside of class time (via readings, audio-recordings, filmed lectures, etc.) rather than through in-class lectures. Class time is then used for discussion, problem-solving, or other hands-on activities, as well as to review more difficult points in the assigned material.

International students in particular often appreciate having additional time to process class material on their own (e.g., by slowing down or rewinding the recorded lectures or assigned YouTube or TED Talk videos) and having more opportunities to apply and extend their learning with support during class time.

There are many excellent online resources for implementing "flipped classroom" approaches; for some of these resources, visit the companion website for this book (www.tesol.org/FISS). Instructors may have access to resources through centers for teaching and learning at their institutions as well.

to participate because of a lack of background knowledge, difficulty with spoken English, or low confidence (see Sidebar 22, Student Perspectives on Participation). Students who come from academic cultures where discussion is not commonly used, as discussed in Chapter 2, may need guidance on the goals for discussion and effective means of engagement. There is a great deal that instructors can do to ensure that all students have the opportunity to deepen their own learning—and that of their peers—through effective engagement in class discussion. We also need to be clear with students on how we are "grading" their participation in class discussion, a point discussed further in Chapter 4 and in Appendix E.

Providing Scaffolding During Classroom Discussions

Be transparent about goals and expectations. One way we can lay the groundwork and create buy-in for class discussion is to be clear with students about our purposes. This sort of transparency is particularly helpful for students who have less experience with peer-to-peer conversation in class and may be intimidated or confused by the prospect. Some of the learning goals we might hope to achieve via class discussion include the following:

- to review and apply course concepts and skills
- to connect new course learning to our past learning or lived experiences
- to invite a range of perspectives on an issue or a case study
- to delve into controversial questions
- to build a sense of community in class

Explaining to students what the goals are for the interaction can help clarify the purpose and establish expectations for how to engage. For example, if the goal is to have deep dialogue that makes space for each student's experience or perspective, we may seat the class in a circle or use a talking piece to ensure that everyone has an opportunity to contribute. There may be other norms we share with students— perhaps we can even cocreate them during class! (See Shapiro, 2022, and Weimer, 2013, for more ideas.) If debate is the goal, in contrast, we may assign roles or perspectives in advance and use a structure that allows for points, counterpoints, and rebuttals.

22

Student Perspectives on Participation

"I was so worried [that] nobody's going to understand my English. I was, like, scared to raise my hand."
—*Student from Brazil*

"I wanted to say something in class, but I was so scared [because] . . . my English sounds so . . . different from native speakers."
—*Student from Japan*

Use a variety of groupings and combinations. Many students are more likely to contribute in pairs or small groups than they are to a discussion that involves the entire class. It can be helpful to begin a discussion with smaller groupings, then have a debrief and expanded discussion with the larger group. One way to ensure that all students stay engaged is to assign roles during small-group discussions (e.g., note-taker, moderator, timekeeper, and reporter—the latter being the one who summarizes the small-group conversation during the debrief). International students may choose less-vocal roles at first, but we can ask that they shift jobs as the semester progresses.

Create a task for students to complete during or after the discussion. This type of task helps increase participation and attention. For example, we could ask students to complete a "1-minute paper" on a note card after the discussion, noting a few highlights, responses, questions, or points of confusion. Students can share their cards with a partner or submit them to us for participation credit. Points from these cards can be the focus of the next lesson or can be posted online.

Sidebar 23, Strategies for Participating in Class Discussions, can be shared with students to provide additional scaffolding for their participation.

Encouraging Interaction in Class Discussions

Construct small groups carefully. Keep an eye on group formation in classes with fewer international students than domestic students so that the former are not isolated from the rest of the class or from their international peers. It can be helpful to encourage a balance of genders and personality types as well in the groupings. We may wish to let students form their own groups, but this approach may result in exclusion or self-segregation. We recommend a balance between teacher-formed and student-formed groupings.

Model effective facilitation, in keeping with the goals. Rather than simply observing the discussion, we can help deepen student engagement and learning by repeating or rephrasing student contributions, highlighting key themes, and inviting students to pause and reflect from time to time. As we facilitate, we should keep in mind the need for wait time between asking a question and calling on students to respond. (Instructors often underestimate how much processing time students need before they are ready to respond to a question or comment.) As the course continues, we may invite students to share the responsibility for facilitation by serving as discussion leaders, time-keepers, moderators, or commentators.

Reward active listening as well as speaking. As we touched on in Chapter 2, U.S. academic culture often places more value on speaking than on listening. We can be more culturally and linguistically inclusive by making clear to students that *both* are crucial parts of effective discussion. In our syllabi, we can note, for example, that students' participation grades involve quality of interaction, not just the number of times they speak. It can be helpful for all students to highlight some of the visible behaviors that indicate

---

23

Strategies for Participating in Class Discussions

Participating in class can be difficult for some students, for a variety of reasons. Here are some strategies we can share with students.

How to Join

Don't always wait to be called on; try using your breath and body language to join the conversation.

If you would like the instructor to call on you, let them know in advance, as many instructors expect students to volunteer themselves.

Types of Comments You Might Make

Link two people's contributions (e.g., "It's interesting that Ming and Lea both seem to . . .").

Explain why you found another person's ideas interesting or useful and describe why (e.g., "I agree with David's point about _____ because in my experience . . .").

Build on another student's comment (e.g., "Building on what Sara was saying, I think . . ."; "Another example of what Ahmed is talking about is . . .").

How to Disagree

Disagree in a respectful and constructive way, noting what is interesting or compelling before countering (e.g., "I think Yazmin brings up an important point. At the same time . . .").

Ask a question that invites further explanation or alternative views (e.g., "Marco, it sounds like you're saying _____ But I wonder whether . . .").

---

engaged listening, such as avoiding using electronic devices (unless necessary for learning needs or goals), using open and receptive body language, and linking one comment to comments made by others. We also encourage students to "cite" one another as sources in their writing.

Monitor group dynamics closely. It is useful to pay attention to who is dominating the discussion and who might be hesitant to join the conversation. While students work in smaller groups, we can mill about and listen to how they interact. If we notice that international students do not get enough talk time, we can invite them into the conversation more explicitly, at that moment or in future class sessions. We can ask all students to reflect regularly on ways they can "step up" or "step back" in order to equalize spoken contributions. Raichle introduces "Three Then Me" in her classes, which asks contributing students to allow three peers to speak before they make another comment. This is usually directed implicitly at "dominant" students as a strategy for sharing the floor with others. (We return to the topic of group dynamics in Chapter 4 when providing guidance on supporting group projects and other collaborative work.)

Facilitating Noticing During Class Discussion

Highlight possibilities for elaboration or clarification. Our responses to student contributions provide clues about which comments are partially incorrect, incomplete, or confusing. International students will also learn from our modeling how to ask for an explanation or elicit more information. We can demonstrate how to ask for clarification ("Could you say that again in another way?" or "I think what you are saying is___. Is that accurate?"), ask for elaboration ("Can you say a little more about that?"), or solicit contrasting opinions ("Who could offer an alternative perspective on this?" or "Who might like to summarize or even role-play another perspective?"). This technique of strategic questioning is what Loretta Ross (2019) frames as "calling in," which, she argues, is a better alternative to "calling out" because the latter often has a chilling effect on student discussion. As a reminder, in Chapter 2, we included examples of difficult scenarios, including ones that might emerge in class discussion, along with possible responses. For clarification related to language comprehension, see the tips in Sidebar 24, Requesting Clarification From Students.

Create opportunities for meta-conversation. Take time to ask students what they have observed in discussion (e.g., themes, patterns, dynamics, etc.). One activity that works well for this meta-level reflection is a "Fishbowl Conversation," in which one group of students sits in a circle, engaging in discussion, while the others sit in a larger circle around them, taking notes on the interaction and reflecting on their observations. The groups can then switch roles for the next discussion topic. A more structured (and game-like) version of this that Raichle adapted from the K–12 context is the "Socratic Smackdown." As the discussants engage with their topic, the observers use a scorecard to note behaviors they deem effective (e.g., polite disagreement) or ineffective (e.g., interruptions). For details on this activity, visit the companion website for this book (www.tesol.org/FISS).

Encourage self-reflection. Students can evaluate their own participation in class discussion by identifying what they feel they are doing well and reflecting on whether there might be areas for improvement (e.g., "Could I step up or step back more in the conversation?"). Students can also share suggestions for how to adjust the discussion structure or norms in order to equalize participation. These reflections can be done during class or outside as a free-write, a structured reflection, or an online survey.

Raise student awareness of the various genres of speaking. It is useful to consider the various modes or media in which class discussions can take place and—where possible—to provide students with a few options for engaging. In addition to the collaborative reading and note-taking strategies discussed earlier, students may be invited to join online discussions (synchronous or asynchronous), share comments on social media, or record (either as an audio or video recording) their responses to a prompt or text (e.g., using a class Flip assignment; see www.flip. com). Moreover, there are other modes in which students can speak with each other, by giving mini-presentations, conducting peer interviews, or setting up roundtables or poster sessions. In Chapter 4, we will see more examples as part of our discussion of assignments and assessment.

Promoting Growth Mindset and Lifelong Language Learning

In the final section of this chapter, we wish to return to the concept of language acquisition to provide some strategies that help all students (and instructors) continue to grow as language learners. It is useful to keep in mind that it often takes at least 5 to 7 years of consistent study and use of a language for a language learner to be "on par" with proficient speakers of that language—and sometimes 10 years or more for older learners (Collier, 1989; Krashen et al., 1979).

We are sometimes asked by international students what they can do to continue improving their English, beyond the work expected for our courses. Many think that if they simply complete a grammar workbook or memorize a list of new vocabulary, they will improve their ability to communicate effectively in English. In fact, what best facilitates continued language acquisition for advanced learners is increased input and feedback. Hence, we encourage students to read more nonacademic or general-

---

24

Requesting Clarification From Students

Many instructors dread the moment when they do not understand what a student is saying. It may be tempting to use the "smile and nod" technique to avoid awkwardness, but this is unhelpful to students in the long run. Here are some kind ways to solicit clarification:

- **Use "I" statements.** For instance, say, "I'm sorry—could you repeat that? I couldn't hear you very well."

- **Ask for explanation.** Ask the student to expand on their comment, perhaps rephrasing or giving an example.

- **Request that the student write it down.** If needed, ask the student to write down a word or phrase, if pronunciation of just one word or phrase is hindering your comprehension.

- **Encourage peer assistance.** Where appropriate, it can be helpful to invite a peer, particularly one from a similar language background to help clarify, if possible.

- **Maintain friendly, relaxed body language.** Try to avoid expressing frustration or displeasure at the situation, as this might hinder students from making another attempt to communicate. Remember that confusion is normal and that it is the students' learning—and that of their classmates—that matters most.

Once we do clarify, we should restate the comment or question to make sure everyone understands. It may be useful to repeat the word or phrase that was most challenging, as often it is one that does not follow phonetic spelling rules.

---

audience texts (e.g., newspapers, blogs, novels, or short stories) and participate in conversation groups or other extracurricular activities that require frequent use of conversational English. Sidebar 25, Language Learning Strategies, provides insights into why these priorities are helpful for long-term language development.

We do occasionally point students to online resources for practice in particular skills. For some of our favorite online resources, visit the companion website for this book (www.tesol.org/FISS), and we may highlight strategies that can support students in meeting their personal goals for language learning (see Sidebars 25 and 26). We also encourage international students to explore cocurricular opportunities that allow them to use language in new ways. Activities such as student government or other leadership roles, employment with residential life, community service or engagement, and academic tutoring (e.g., with writing and learning centers or world language programs) can benefit students academically, linguistically, *and* socially, as we will discuss further in Chapter 5.

We also remind students that continuing to maintain and develop their home languages is important to their academic success and overall multilingual competence (Dolas et al., 2022; Jessner, 2018; Yamashita, 2002). In other words, it is unnecessary—and can be harmful, in fact—for international students to adopt an "English-only" approach during their time abroad. Maintaining one's home language(s) in fact helps students continue feeling connected to their ethnic, cultural, and geographic communities during their time abroad.

In fact, as we noted at the beginning of this chapter, we try to highlight for *all of our students* the many benefits of multilingualism. In an increasingly interconnected world, it is a tremendous asset to be able to interact with individuals from a variety of language backgrounds. To this end, Sidebar 26, Communicating Across Language Differences, offers some strategies for effective communication across language or dialect differences. We can also find ways to highlight and build on the strengths and contributions that multilingual students bring to the classroom and to our institutions at large. This is a topic we will consider further in Chapter 5.

25

Language Learning Strategies

Articles and blogs highlight a range of language learning strategies supported by research in second language acquisition. Here are some strategies that we promote among students. See Oxford (2017) and Wong and Nunan (2011) for more on language learning strategies.

- Set clear and realistic goals and monitor these goals frequently.

- Find ways to foster and sustain your motivation.

- Harness moments throughout the day for learning—watch a video, listen to a podcast, review flashcards, read and review academic articles, write a summary of content, and so on.

- Take advantage of resources available to you through the library, internet, academic support services, and the community.

- Identify a conversation partner or study buddy to build accountability, and practice together often.

- Develop communicative strategies to employ when messages break down and you need clarification.

- Let go of perfection. Take risks and make mistakes, as this is how we learn!

Conclusion: Toward Effective Assignments and Other Assessment

It is beyond the scope of this chapter to delve deeply into all of the potential instructional situations in which we might apply principles of SLA to make our instruction more linguistically inclusive. However, it is our hope that the scaffolding-interaction-noticing framework we have presented in this chapter provides instructors with a lens through which to consider all of their pedagogical decision-making. Analyzing our pedagogical choices through the lens of this framework will help ensure that we are supporting international students—indeed, all students—in doing their best work. Although we may not think of ourselves as language teachers, there is a great deal we can do to support our students' learning and use of academic language and literacy, including of the terms and concepts central to our disciplines. We can also consider how to be more culturally and linguistically inclusive in our assignments and assessment measures. In Chapter 4, we offer strategies for crafting and evaluating assignments, designing and facilitating exams, and responding to and evaluating student work. As we talk about assignments and assessment, we will be building on the guidance that we presented in this chapter and in Chapter 2.

Communicating Across Language Differences   26

Here are some helpful reminders about communicating with students (or others) from different language backgrounds:

- Spoken accent is not the best indicator of communicative ability. Someone who began learning English as an adolescent or adult may continue to have an accent that sounds foreign, but the person can still be highly proficient in the language.

- Speaking loudly does not make one's message clearer or more comprehensible. Speaking a bit more slowly, using visual and written cues, and checking for understanding are much more helpful strategies for improving communication.

- Many gestures (e.g., shrugging, making the "okay" sign, motioning to "come here") are not universal. Hence, they may complicate, rather than simplify, communication.

- Most language learners want to know if what they are saying is unclear. Do not pretend to understand (e.g., by smiling and nodding). Instead, ask for clarification using other strategies (see Sidebar 24, Requesting Clarification From Students).

- Many language learners appreciate corrective feedback on pronunciation, grammar, and other aspects of language. However, it is a good idea to ask whether an individual wants this feedback before you provide it.

- The ability to communicate with users of multiple languages and dialects is a learned skill that all of us can improve over time.

CHAPTER 4

Effective and Equitable Assignments and Assessments

Assignment design and other assessment practices are two topics that instructors and administrators often ask us about in workshops and consultations—and for good reason, as these aspects of our pedagogy allow us to gauge student learning and map out future instruction. But assignments and assessment can be fraught topics as well: Students often report heightened levels of stress around completing assigned work and receiving feedback and grades on exams and other assessments. Instructors might experience tension around these topics as well, particularly when students misunderstand the goal or expectations for an assignment, submit work that is incomplete or difficult to comprehend, or perhaps do not submit anything at all!

One of our goals in this chapter is to address how to respond to—and even prevent—some of these challenges. But we also want to empower faculty to see assignments and assessment as an opportunity for dialogue and relationship-building, in keeping with our values of *access* and *asset*. Our assignments and assessments can even be a source of excitement and joy when they are structured, scaffolded, and evaluated effectively. It can be incredibly gratifying, for example, to see evidence of students' deep learning, innovative application, or skills development from one assignment or unit to the next. Thus, although this chapter presents assignments and assessment strategies that are particularly effective with international students, it can, we hope, help reconnect us to our passion for student learning and growth—the thing that brought most of us to this profession in the first place!

Before we delve in, we wish to recognize that "assignments" and "assessment" are distinct but overlapping topics. Some parts of this chapter focus on one more than the other, but the two are connected enough that we (the authors) felt it was useful to address them in a single chapter. In the following section, we share some foundational information about assessment before moving on to specific strategies for assignment and assessment design and implementation.

(See Sidebar 27, Summative Assessments: Pros and Cons.)

Summative Assessments: Pros and Cons

In-Class Exam

Pros: These exams are commonly used, reliable, and relatively easy to facilitate.

Cons: Time constraints may put international students at a disadvantage. These may not measure deeper learning, such as critical thinking and application of concepts. Also, many students experience test anxiety.

Take-Home Exam

Pros: Time constraints are less of an issue. Students can be expected to do more critical thinking and reflection.

Cons: These exams may make it difficult to measure acquired knowledge because all students have access to course materials and other sources.

Term Paper or Essay

Pros: Writing about course content can both deepen and demonstrate student learning. This assessment can also allow students to improve their written communication skills.

Cons: Students may procrastinate and not produce their best work at the end of the term. Grading and providing feedback can be time-consuming for the instructor—especially when assessing the work of students writing in an additional language.

Portfolio

Pros: Portfolios show growth over time and promote student reflection.

Cons: Students may resist not receiving grades on early drafts of their work.

Oral Presentation

Pros: Presentations may be easier for students than writing a full paper. They allow students to learn from one another and practice academic speaking.

Cons: Presentations can be challenging for students who are not confident with public speaking. Presentations can also take up a lot of class time, unless they are recorded outside of class.

Explaining Assessment and Why It Matters

Although assessment has been defined in a variety of ways, the working definition we employ here is that assessment is any means of measuring what students have learned. Although instructors in some disciplines may use preliminary assessments for other purposes, such as to place students into courses (e.g., diagnostic tests in mathematics and world languages), most of the assessment we do in higher education is designed to gauge student learning.

For many instructors, exams are the first form of assessment that comes to mind. Indeed, exams are a common form of assessment in higher education—particularly in certain disciplines and for certain groups of students (e.g., in large introductory lecture courses). However, we will address many other types of assessment in this chapter as well.

There are two general categories of assessment—summative and formative. Summative assessment is designed to evaluate student learning at the end of a unit of study. Summative assessments tend to be more time-consuming for the student to complete and for the instructor to grade. (See Sidebar 27, Summative Assessments: Pros and Cons.) They usually constitute a large part of the course grade, which is one reason they often create more stress for students (Cassady & Johnson, 2002; Nilson, 2016). Another cause of stress is that summative assessments are often timed, if they are completed during class. This can create a barrier to success for international students who use English as an additional language and may not work as quickly as other groups. (We will return to the issue of timed assessments later in this chapter.)

Formative assessment, on the other hand, is usually low stakes (or at least lower stakes) and is designed to not only measure student learning but also facilitate the learning process itself. Instructors can use results from formative assessment to guide their future instruction, answering questions such as these:

- How are students connecting with my course concepts and materials?

- Where are there gaps in student understanding or skills?

- Are we ready to move on, or do we need more review or practice with the material in this unit?

- What seems to be working well in my instruction, and where might I make changes in order to increase student learning and confidence?

Formative assessment usually takes place with greater frequency and throughout the term, so we can make changes midway through the course to enhance student learning. Some of the most common examples of formative assessment are

- practice exercises, problem sets, or other homework assignments;

- group application and review activities;

- "writing-to-learn" assignments, such as journals, response papers, free-writes, exit tickets, or other reflective writing;

- take-home quizzes (sometimes self-graded);

- online discussion; and

- peer review or other work with early drafts of papers and projects.

Nilson (2016) points out that many of these activities can be used during class as a way to gain in-the-moment insight into what students are learning and where there might be gaps in their understanding or skills. Many of the activity ideas presented in Chapter 3 serve this function, providing valuable feedback for our instruction while also keeping students engaged in learning. Formative assessments are often graded less stringently than summative assessments—sometimes with a simple system that indicates whether work is below, at, or exceeding expectations (e.g., ✓+, ✓, ✓-).

Research suggests that the most equitable and effective way to assess student learning is through a multipronged approach that includes a combination of formative and summative measures distributed throughout the semester (e.g., Bryan & Clegg, 2019; Hundley & Kahn, 2019). A multipronged approach gives students many opportunities to show what they know and can do, particularly if some of the assessments are completed early in the term (i.e., "front-loaded," as will be discussed further). Assessment early in the course offers valuable feedback to students and instructors so that both can make changes in time to increase learning and performance. Studies have found, in fact, that placing greater emphasis on formative assessment helps improve retention and achievement for students who struggle academically (e.g., Irons & Elkington, 2021; Koka, 2017).

Guiding Principles for Assessment and Assignment Design

Before delving into strategies for assignments and assessment, we wish to highlight some of the principles that inform this work. As we touched on earlier, our approach is grounded in the values of access and asset. One way to hold true to those values is to be intentional about what we want students to learn and how we will measure that learning. This means that we need to articulate clear and measurable outcomes for each course (or unit) and then design assignments and other assessment measures that can reflect student achievement of (and growth toward) those outcomes. We then structure the rest of the course or unit to build up to those assignments and assessments. Wiggins and McTighe (2005) call this process "Backward Design" (see also Fink, 2003; Mills et al., 2019). We have found this approach to be one of the best ways to ensure our goals are aligned with our assignments and assessment practices.

We can also be intentional in thinking through ways to recognize and draw on student assets through our assignments and assessments, including global perspectives, cultural backgrounds, and linguistic resources. Here are some suggestions for doing so, picking up on points we have discussed in Chapters 2 and 3:

- Ask students to apply course concepts and methods to texts, case studies, or data sets from outside the United States.

- Make space for students to reference their own lived experiences in some of their writing or other work.

- Identify ways in which our disciplinary norms and course materials have been shaped by geographic or cultural context, and encourage students to critique ethnocentrism when they see it.

- Invite students to find and cite (or share) sources in languages other than English or even to incorporate other languages, dialects, or styles into their writing, where appropriate.

Being intentional with ourselves prepares us to be transparent with students about our goals, expectations, procedures, and feedback. This transparency helps them understand what they are learning and why, as well as how they are expected to demonstrate that learning. As we will explore later in this chapter, there are many ways to increase transparency in our instructions, grading tools (e.g., rubrics and checklists), and modeling of student work.

Another value that shapes how we think about assignments and assessment is equity. A commitment to equity means that we recognize that different students may need different kinds of support. In other words, fairness does not necessarily mean giving students the "same" treatment (Silva, 1997; Tardy & Whittig, 2017). This does not mean that we tailor our assignments or assessment practices to fit each individual, though; rather, we try to build in options, structures, and resources that might benefit a range of students, perhaps for a variety of reasons (language background, learning differences, etc.). Throughout this chapter, as we have done throughout this book, we will highlight how strategies and opportunities that are particularly helpful for international students can benefit everyone. This is the central principle behind Universal or Inclusive Design, which we will return to later in this chapter (see also Rao & Torres, 2017).

A final insight that underlies the guidance in this chapter is that assessment and feedback can be forms of relationship-building with and among our students.

Many instructors prioritize building positive relationships with students but sometimes forget that assignments and other assessments are part of that relationship. Establishing clear expectations for exams, papers, and other assessments helps students feel respected and confident (e.g., Lin & Scherz, 2014), and providing feedback that is fair, clear, and constructive will reinforce students' developing identities as members of our academic communities (Duff, 2010; Lee & Orgill, 2022). When we invite students to assess themselves, each other, and our own instruction, we further reinforce their sense of community and belonging in our classrooms.

Here are the questions we will address in the remainder of this chapter:

1. How is assessment shaped by academic culture?

2. How can we design and scaffold assessments effectively?

3. How can we minimize cultural and linguistic bias in exams and assignments?

4. What are best practices for providing feedback, including feedback on language?

5. What are the most equitable approaches to grading and evaluation of student work?

6. What other issues and questions often emerge in relation to assessment, especially in relation to international students?

Assessment and Academic Culture

As we discussed in Chapter 2, many of our instructional practices are shaped by cultural values that we may or may not recognize as such. Academic culture is like water we are swimming in but do not always talk about explicitly. (Recall the tale of the frog and the fish from Chapter 2.)

When it comes to assessment, differences in academic cultures can be quite pronounced. At many institutions around the world, students may be graded primarily or exclusively on a single summative assessment at the end of the term, often an oral or written exam. Thus, international students studying in the United States are sometimes surprised to find that course grades are often based on a much wider set of criteria, including "class participation," which is often poorly defined (though it does not have to be, as we discussed in Chapter 3).

Here are some of the other assessment features that might be unfamiliar to international students at U.S. institutions:

- There is less value placed on memorization and recall and more emphasis on analysis, argumentation, and critique—additional criteria that U.S. instructors often expect but rarely define.

- U.S. institutions are more likely to incorporate frequent use of collaborative learning both during and outside of class (e.g., group projects and presentations; teamwork in labs or other experiential learning; preassigned study groups for homework or exam preparation).

- Institutions in the United States use letter grades (A through F, except E) and grade point averages (GPAs) out of 4.0, in contrast with other grading systems and class rankings. For resources that provide a window into the range of grading systems in higher education worldwide, visit the companion website for this book (www.tesol.org/FISS).

Academic culture also shapes expectations for writing, which we explored in Chapter 2 and will return to later in this chapter. Recognizing that our international students—and likely many domestic students as well—might come to us with a range of views and experiences with assessment, we must offer clear assessment goals, expectations, and policies. Next, we discuss how we can be more intentional and transparent when it comes to our assignments and other assessments.

Designing and Scaffolding Assessments

There are a number of steps we can take to ensure that our assessment is aligned with our pedagogical goals and reflects our commitment to access and asset. These steps are in many ways an elaboration on the Backward Design approach mentioned earlier.

Identify Measurable Learning Goals

If the goal of assessment is to measure student learning, then it is important that we match each assignment, activity, or other assessment to the specific learning goals it aims to measure. As we alluded to in Sidebar 27 on summative assessments, certain types of assessments are better matched to certain kinds of learning outcomes. For example, an instructor who wants to measure students' ability to think critically about a primary source text or an empirical research article may find that a multiple-choice quiz does not allow for that level of analysis. Similarly, an instructor who wants to know if each student has acquired the skill set to solve a particular kind of problem may not glean that information from a group project, as it can be difficult to determine what role each student played in solving the problem.

Work Backward From Our Goals

As we mentioned earlier, assessment is most effective when it is integrated throughout the course, rather than only at the end. With a "Backward Design" approach, the instructor first determines the learning outcomes for the entire course, then maps those outcomes to appropriate assignments and assessments that will measure student success in achieving those outcomes. Finally, the instructor develops a learning plan that builds up to those assignments and assessments. To implement this Backward Design approach effectively, instructors need to be able to break a larger task or product into smaller assignments, develop a clear timeline of what needs to be accomplished at various points in the semester, and offer feedback and support throughout the process. While this process definitely requires time and energy, it usually results in better outcomes and fewer cases of student panic, frustration, and failure (Tomaš & Shapiro, 2021; to read the full article, visit the companion website for this book at www.tesol.org/FISS).

Here are two examples of what this Backward Design process might look like. We have noted use of the strategies presented in Chapter 3 (scaffolding, interaction, and noticing) in each scenario.

- A science, technology, engineering, and mathematics (STEM) instructor wants students to be able to deliver poster presentations at an upcoming research symposium. To build up to this assignment, the instructor first has students examine posters from previous semesters to get a feel for the genre, highlighting structure, linguistic choices, and citation practices (scaffolding, noticing). Students then begin working on the content and layout for their posters, using templates and other resources (e.g., handouts on citation style) provided by the instructor (scaffolding). They engage in peer review of early poster drafts, in person or electronically, and work in groups to practice sharing highlights from their posters orally (interaction). The instructor provides a set of questions for them to address as they talk about their work (scaffolding): What did you do for your research? What did you find? Why does it matter?

- An instructor in the humanities wants students to be able to analyze a primary source (e.g., an artistic work, literary text, or historical document) using a theoretical framework or approach from class. The instructor first provides students with a checklist of the central components of the assignment: (i) a detailed description or summary of the work they are analyzing, (ii) an overview of the theoretical concepts or framework, and (iii) the findings and implications from their original analysis (scaffolding). To build up to this final paper, students might discuss published analyses of other works (interaction, noticing), practice analyzing artifacts in class (scaffolding, interaction), and submit a proposal or rationale before undertaking their original analysis (scaffolding). They may submit some sections of the paper (e.g., the introduction and the theoretical framework) for early feedback—or peer review (interaction)—before they turn in a full draft.

In both of these examples, the instructor has developed a challenging summative assessment that measures student learning and mastery. However, students build up gradually to that larger assessment so they have the clarity, confidence, and skill set necessary to produce high-quality work. Providing clear expectations, samples of work, scaffolding activities and resources, and opportunities for noticing and interaction with and among students helps ensure that everyone has what they need to be successful in meeting the instructor's high expectations.

The following sections share other strategies illustrated in these scenarios.

Distribute Assessments More Evenly Across the Term

Many instructors place a lot of emphasis on exams, papers, or projects submitted at the end of the term. However, these final "products" may not reflect students' best work, in part because students have so many major assignments due in the same time span. This tendency to "end load" (versus "front load") our assessment creates even more of a challenge for international students who use English as an additional language because it often takes these students considerably longer to complete academic work (Lin & Scherz, 2014; Stoynoff, 1997).

There are a number of other advantages to distributing major assignments and other assessments across the term. First, we can receive timely and frequent information about how students are performing, so we can be proactive in offering additional instruction and support. Second, students often produce better work earlier in the semester, when they are more motivated and have greater physical and mental energy. Third, giving students more work earlier on helps prevent grading "burnout" at the end of the semester, when many instructors feel overwhelmed by stacks of high-stakes papers or exams. And finally, if we do less "cramming" of summative assessments at the end of the term, there will be more space for students to synthesize and reflect on what they have learned, which can help promote deep and transferable learning for students and provide us with valuable insights into how we can improve our course in the next iteration.

Provide Explicit Instructions and Guidelines

Because we (the authors) work closely with our institutions' writing and learning centers, we have an on-the-ground view of the sorts of assignments that are most overwhelming for international students. We have found that in many cases, it is not academic rigor but a *lack of clarity* that makes an assignment difficult (see Chapter 3). Research has shown that international students are particularly appreciative of detailed assignment instructions (Lin & Scherz, 2014). See Sidebar 28, Improving Clarity of Instructions, for examples of instructions that could be improved.

As we discussed earlier, the learning goals of an assignment need to be clear to us and to our students. Without this clarity, students may focus on *quantity* rather than *quality* in their work. For example, they may try to "cram" as much information as possible into a single response in order to show they have done their reading or research, rather than choosing the information that best suits their purposes. Students may miss opportunities for original analysis or creative expression as well if they do not understand our intentions and expectations.

Students who know why they are doing an assignment and what the instructor is looking for are much less anxious—and much more likely to be successful. It is also important to keep in mind that the norms for academic work (e.g., how arguments are constructed, how secondary sources are used) differ across academic cultures, as we discuss later in this chapter. Therefore, clarity about expectations is even more important for international students who have less experience with U.S. academic culture and may not be familiar with the rhetorical conventions of a particular genre or discipline (see Chapter 2 for more on this topic).

For major assignments, it is helpful to provide instructions—ideally in writing—that include the following details:

- **Purpose and goals.** Why are students being asked to complete this assignment at this point in the semester? How does it deepen or evaluate their learning?

- **Audience, genre, and format.** To whom will students be presenting their work? What are they producing (e.g., "research paper" vs. "project proposal" vs. "summary or response paper"), and what does it typically look like?

- **Grading priorities.** What is most important for students to include or do in this assignment? What will we emphasize in the evaluation of student work?

- **Process and timeline.** What parts or aspects of the assignment are likely to be the most challenging? What are the steps students should take to succeed on this assignment? What is a reasonable timeline for work? How should feedback from their peers and the instructor be incorporated into the final draft or the next assignment?

- **Challenges, resources, and support.** What tend to be the most challenging aspects of this assignment? Where can students go for help? What role do we (instructors) play in supporting students, compared with other entities, such as the writing and learning center, libraries, and other supports?

- **Opportunities and options.** Are there multiple forms the assignment might take? If so, how might students choose from the available options? Where might they be able to draw on their cultural and linguistic assets? For example, can they reference work from scholars outside the United States or incorporate sources written in languages other than English? Could they draw on their intercultural or global competence to provide a fresh perspective? (See Chapter 5 for more possibilities.)

We can employ the scaffolding-interaction-noticing framework when planning delivery of instructions and expectations for an assignment. For example, it is important that we not only review this information in class but also provide it in written form (scaffolding), given that listening comprehension can be a challenge for some international students. It is also useful to give students time to process written instructions in class (scaffolding, interaction, noticing), to ask questions (noticing), to brainstorm possibilities and troubleshoot potential challenges as a group (interaction), and so forth. Providing grading rubrics or checklists (scaffolding) as part of the instructions for an assignment is another excellent way to make our goals and priorities more transparent (noticing), as is discussed in more detail later in this chapter.

Model Both Process and Product

Many international students appreciate learning about the process by which they should complete an assignment or activity, in addition to knowing what the product should look like. One way to help students with this is to do a "think aloud" in class to articulate how we might complete a task or solve a problem. Restating the expectations in the form of giving advice (e.g., "I would most likely start by ___ and then I would ___, but I wouldn't ___") helps personalize the assignment and gives students concrete steps for how to begin. For less familiar assignments, such as oral presentations, we can provide opportunities for students to view and reflect on successful examples.

For example, in modeling expectations for an oral presentation assignment, we could incorporate the following activities:

- Show a video of a prior student presentation (with permission) and have students evaluate it with the rubric we intend to use for their presentations.

- Invite former students back to present their projects to the class or to share about their experiences, including demonstrating how to handle questions from the audience.

- Show a video clip of a brief presentation relevant to our discipline. Following the clip, discuss the presentation and presenter qualities that were effective or ineffective (e.g., body language, organization, amount of text on slides, eye contact, humor, rate of speech).

Visit www.ted.com for an excellent collection of presentations on a range of topics and by speakers of many language backgrounds. For a sample assignment from one author (Raichle's) public speaking course using this resource, visit the companion site for this book (www.tesol.org/FISS).

Many students also find it helpful to see examples of the particular genre or style of work we are asking them to produce. Although some instructors try to use samples from published writers or from students at other institutions, many find it helpful to share work from their own students, past or current. There are some considerations to keep in mind, however, if we do choose to share student work with others:

- Ask permission from the student; also invite them to be named or to remain anonymous.

- Make time to discuss the samples in class or to provide annotations so that students know what you want them to notice in the models.

- Focus on strengths rather than only critiques, and encourage students to do the same. This aspect is important because students who see someone else's work being "ripped apart" (even if it's presented anonymously) often become worried that their own work might be treated in the same way.

- Keep in mind both access and asset: Rather than simply choosing the paper that received the highest grade, we may select an above-average example (or even an excerpt) that feels more within reach for most students. We often intentionally choose examples from multilingual writers—even if those examples include some grammatical errors or inconsistencies (see more on "written accent" later in this chapter)—to illustrate that success for this assignment is not about showing "grammatical perfection" but about demonstrating learning.

One other aspect that should be clear in our instructions, processes, and models of student work is when and how students might draw on secondary sources in their writing. When we articulate expectations and processes for source use, we decrease the likelihood of unintentional instances of plagiarism (see the section Plagiarism or Unconventional Source Use later in this chapter).

Minimizing Cultural and Linguistic Bias

As we discussed in Chapter 2 and earlier in this chapter, cultural background knowledge often factors into higher education teaching and learning in unexpected ways. When designing assignments and assessments, it is important to keep in mind that we want to target the knowledge and skills associated with the course material—not students' assumed cultural knowledge. (This concept of targeting the appropriate knowledge and learning in assessment is called *validity*.)

In Chapter 2, we noted that assignment descriptions are sometimes informed by implicit cultural assumptions (e.g., a letter to a family member might be written in a relatively informal style in one academic culture but more formally in a culture where one is expected to use formal register with elders). This is just one of the ways that cultural bias might influence our assignment or exam prompts. Here are some other examples:

- A history or political science instructor may ask students to compare a historical event or issue they have been studying with one that would be familiar to most domestic students (e.g., the U.S. Civil War) but not necessarily to international students.

- A STEM instructor may include a word problem that assumes knowledge of the English system of measurement (e.g., feet, yards, etc.), which can be unfair to students from countries that use the metric system (i.e., most of the world!).

- An economics or business instructor might ask a question that assumes basic knowledge about the U.S. currency system or stock market.

- A literature instructor might ask students to analyze dialect use in a text without providing the necessary background on which language varieties are represented and what the prevalent attitudes are toward those varieties.

These are just a few examples of how differences in cultural knowledge might make it more difficult for international students to demonstrate what they have learned in our exams, assignments, or other assessments. Although we may not always catch these issues in our work, it is worth considering whether cultural knowledge might have played a role in an international student's work on an exam, essay, or other assignment.

Linguistic bias can come into play as well: For example, there is a well-known mathematics puzzle about a *hound* and a *hare*, which may cause confusion for international students, because those two words are not particularly common in English (compared with *dog* and *rabbit*). Similarly, an English literature essay prompt might ask whether a particular character should be considered a villain. A student who does not know the word *villain*—but does know the work of literature being addressed—may be disadvantaged by this question.

Although we cannot always anticipate these linguistic challenges, we can remind students that we are happy to answer any questions about language, and we can ask students explicitly for clarification on their work when needed. Sidebar 29,

Linguistic Misunderstandings, discusses two examples of misunderstandings that would have persisted if neither the student nor the instructor had taken the time to ask for clarification.

Other Considerations for Quizzes and Exams

Because most test-taking requires a high level of linguistic competence, as well as strict time limits, many international students experience acute test anxiety (e.g., Gerwing et al., 2015; Szafranski et al., 2012). Test anxiety can hinder students' ability to demonstrate what they know and prevents instructors from receiving valuable feedback on student learning (Hembree, 1988). Working to minimize cultural and linguistic bias, as discussed earlier in this chapter, is one way to decrease test anxiety. In the section that follows, we offer additional suggestions for alleviating anxiety. (See Gross-Davis, 2009, and Nilson, 2016, for elaboration and additional tips; also see Sidebar 30, Reflection Questions About Exams.)

Test frequently so that each test carries less weight. More frequent testing also means that students (and instructors) receive more frequent feedback. To avoid making testing a stress-inducing experience, some instructors allow students to drop their lowest quiz or test score or use "proxy" grades, telling students what their grade *would have been* if the instructor had used a traditional grading scale.

Incorporate review activities into the course. This can be done through quiz games and tools (e.g., Jeopardy!, Kahoot!, Quizlet), practice tests, or other activities in class or online. We can encourage students to come prepared with questions or topics they want to review and to form study groups together.

Remind students of useful study skills and test-taking strategies. Some campuses offer optional workshops on these topics through learning centers, testing centers, or other academic departments. Advertising these offerings to students can send the message that it is normal to need help in these areas.

Consider letting students help develop the exam. Students can submit potential test questions, either individually or in groups. (This is one type of "1-minute paper," an idea discussed in Chapter 3.) Students whose contributions make it onto the exam will feel particularly gratified!

Give students the opportunity to explain their answers on multiple-choice and true or false questions. This can provide valuable insight into the thinking that went into their responses.

Build the difficulty of questions from easy to difficult. This strategy allows students to "ease into" the test. (We recommend telling students explicitly that this is how you have organized the exam so they can allocate time accordingly.)

Consider using "open-book" assessments. Research has suggested that students may learn more from organizing their notes or writing "crib sheets" (note cards or pieces of paper with key information) than they do from the rote memorization (i.e., "cramming") they might do the night before an exam (e.g., Green et al., 2016).

Leave space for students to construct one additional question they wish to answer on the exam. This approach allows students to demonstrate learning of material that may not have been captured on the exam. It may also give us ideas of items to include in future iterations of the exam!

Solicit students' feedback on quizzes and exams. Students appreciate being heard, and their input can go a long way in helping you refine assessments.

Reflection Questions About Exams

30

- What challenges have you experienced while designing exam questions in courses that include large numbers of international students? What accommodations, if any, do you make to reduce test anxiety and increase success for all students?

- Complete the Practice Exercise for Writing Effective Exam Questions (Appendix C). After completing this exercise, turn to a set of your own quiz/exam questions. How might you revise them considering criteria such as clarity, language use, cultural bias, and layout?

Providing Feedback on Student Work

Providing feedback on student work is one of the most labor-intensive parts of our jobs as instructors. Giving good feedback requires a great deal of time, as well as mental and emotional energy—particularly if we are thinking carefully about how our feedback can promote students' learning and growth.

Ultimately, we need to see feedback as an ongoing conversation, a chance to strengthen our relationship with students and their relationships with one another (Shapiro, 2020, 2022).

Next, we discuss some general principles for making the feedback conversation as effective and inclusive as possible, some of which are also referenced in Sidebar 31, Strategies for Providing Effective—and Efficient—Writing Feedback.

Prioritize Timeliness Over Thoroughness

Many instructors delay returning work or providing feedback to students because it takes them so long to respond to each assignment. Students may not receive feedback in time to make adjustments for the next assignment, which they understandably find frustrating. Research shows that student uptake and learning from feedback increase the sooner that feedback is provided—particularly in instances where they have the opportunity to incorporate that feedback into a revised or final draft or into the next assignment or assessment (e.g., Ferris, 1995; Lee, 2013). To provide feedback in a timely manner, we must be selective in what we respond to and how (Shapiro, 2022).

Many instructors assume that students always want more feedback—even if it takes longer. But is more feedback always better? The answer, perhaps surprisingly,

31

**Strategies for Providing Effective—
and Efficient—Writing Feedback**

Build in opportunities for feedback throughout the process. By breaking up a larger assignment into smaller steps and encouraging students to make use of writing centers and peer feedback, instructors can minimize the time spent providing feedback at the end of the assignment.

Stay focused on your goals. Remember your overall objectives for the assignment and comment the most on those. This may mean ignoring certain aspects of language or formatting, particularly if students will not be revising the work.

Remember that more is not always better. Students may be overwhelmed by the amount of feedback they receive. Often, a few comments per page is plenty for them to process. You can always give students the option to request additional feedback, if they wish.

Focus on general trends, but highlight specific examples. Students tend to appreciate "local" feedback, or specific points of strength or weakness in the text more than generalized feedback at the end. Thus, if we provide end comments, it is helpful to highlight instances in the writing that illustrate each general point.

Use a rubric. While rubrics take time to create, they often save time in the grading process, as instructors can easily highlight areas of strength and weakness.

Talk with colleagues. Colleagues often have other creative ways to manage the grading workload—particularly those who teach writing-intensive courses.

is not necessarily. Receiving a lot of feedback can be overwhelming for students, especially when that feedback addresses both general and specific issues at once (Anson, 1989; Harris, 2017). (See Sidebar 31 and the following section for more suggestions.)

Be Intentional and Strategic

As with other aspects of assessment, we need to think carefully about the why, when, and how of our feedback. This is one way that we can prioritize quality (i.e., usefulness or impact) of feedback over quantity. The type, amount, and mode of feedback may vary depending on our goals, the nature of the assignment, and where students are in the process. For example, on a paper or project that students will revise, we usually comment only or primarily on content and organization, realizing that issues of style and mechanics are better addressed later in the writing process. On a piece of work that will not be revised, we may use a grading rubric to capture the strengths and areas for improvement, providing just a few written comments focused on what the student has accomplished and what they might keep in mind for the next assignment.

It is also useful to think strategically about our mode for feedback. Reading handwritten comments can be a challenge for international students who may not be used to reading English handwriting but might be hesitant to ask their instructor for clarification, for fear of seeming disrespectful. It is usually best to type rather than handwrite comments. Some instructors use audio or video recordings as an option for feedback, although some students appreciate the concreteness of margin comments and other written feedback. There are a number of resources we can use to make our written (asynchronous) feedback more accessible and useful to students and that can even allow students to respond directly to specific comments and suggestions! Online collaboration tools like Google Docs and Padlet work well for this. There are some software programs like Eli Review that can help scaffold the feedback process.

Provide Scaffolding During Oral or In-Person Feedback

Many instructors provide feedback for some assignments via one-on-one conferences. These meetings can also strengthen our relationships with students, especially if we take time to ensure the conversations are accessible and useful. Instructors should keep a couple of points in mind with regard to these meetings.

First, it can be both culturally unfamiliar and linguistically challenging for a student to meet individually with an instructor. We may want to offer students the option of meeting in pairs or small groups instead. We can also let them choose whether to meet online or in person (some video-conferencing systems, for example, offer an auto-transcript feature that may be useful for students who struggle with listening comprehension).

Second, retaining information can be difficult for students who use English as an additional language. It is helpful to take time to summarize key takeaways from the conversation or to provide some written feedback before or during the meeting so that students can remember the most important points and next steps. We sometimes invite students to audio-record the meeting if they are struggling, so that they can listen later to make sure they caught everything. If our availability is limited, we can give students a choice between receiving written feedback or having an individual meeting.

Create Opportunities for Students' Self-Reflection

Of course, we are not the only source of feedback. Students can assess themselves and provide feedback to us about their own experience with an assignment. One way to do this is by requiring an "assignment wrapper" (or "writer's memo"; see Shapiro, 2022) alongside the submission of student work. This is a short reflection—usually written, but it could also be audio- or video-recorded—in which students tell us how the process went for them and how they feel about the work they are submitting. We may give students one or two prompts to guide their reflection, such as the following:

- How did the writing and research process go for you on this assignment?

- What was most challenging about this assignment?

- How do you feel about the draft you're submitting? What do you see as its strengths and areas for improvement?

- What would you most like feedback on, and why?

Students often disclose something in these short memos that shifts the feedback we provide to them. For example, a student may share that they did not manage their time well and are aware that the current draft is not yet ready for feedback. In cases like these, it is pointless to spend our time telling students what they already know. Instead, we may invite the student to meet with us to craft a plan for completing the next draft or assignment. We can also remind students of extension policies and options (see the section on extensions later in this chapter) so that we receive work that better demonstrates student learning.

After we have provided a round of feedback to students, it is worthwhile to give them time to process our feedback by reflecting on trends and next steps. Setting aside time for this during class can remind students that our feedback is a resource and part of an ongoing dialogue. We may even assign a short "synthesis" assignment that students complete during or after class so we have a sense of their takeaways from the feedback. It is also helpful to make short meetings available for students to process feedback with us, particularly if we are asking them to revise large portions of their work, which can be daunting for anyone.

Encourage and Support Peer-to-Peer Feedback

Students can also get valuable feedback from their peers. There is a growing body of scholarship on effective approaches and structures for peer review, including for groups that include multilingual and international students. Peer review can be a struggle for international students for several reasons. First, they may have had little practice with peer review (or other collaborative work, as noted earlier) and therefore may be unsure about the goals and best practices. Second, students who have had less experience with U.S. academic culture (or with doing academic coursework in English) may worry that they have less to offer to their classmates— particularly if they think the focus of the review should be on "editing" rather than responding to content (McLeay & Wesson, 2014; Van Rompay-Bartels & Geessink, 2021; Yu & Lee, 2016).

Additionally, it may take longer for some international students to read the work of others, so timing can be an issue (although there is often a wide range of reading skills among domestic students as well, so this is always a potential concern). There is much we can do to ensure all students have a clear understanding of what they are doing and how. Here are some strategies for setting up effective peer review in classes that include international students:

- **Provide clear goals and criteria.** We need to be intentional with students— and with ourselves—about why we are doing peer review for an assignment. Students also need to know what they should focus on, and what they can let go of, in their feedback. (Rubrics can help; see the section on rubrics later in this chapter for more on this topic.) Finally, students need to know whether and how their peer review work will be graded, as we discuss in the rest of this section. One thing to note is that we usually focus peer review on "higher order concerns" such as argument, evidence and examples, and organization, rather than "lower order concerns" such as language, style, and mechanics. This approach helps ensure that multilingual students are seen and treated as equals in the peer review process and prevents students from getting nitpicky with each other's work.

- **Consider the options.** We can vary the length of the peer review to fit our pedagogical goals and constraints. Some instructors use class time to discuss the purpose and procedures for peer review but assign the review itself as homework. Others have students do a short "flash review" session during class, in which each student talks through their main ideas or provides a few comments on their peers' work. Another option to consider is whether students will be asked to read work aloud or just to read silently. Many international students prefer the latter, or they might appreciate hearing their work read aloud by someone else. One additional source of student- to-student feedback, of course, is from peer tutors at writing and learning centers, which we will discuss further in Chapter 5.

- **Structure and model the process.** Some students may not have had experience with peer review before, so it is helpful to provide tips and tools for being timely and effective with feedback. We often use checklists, rubrics, or other guidelines so students focus on our priorities. For example, in a short, in-class peer review, students might be asked to provide the writer with one strength or point of learning, one question or area for improvement, and one suggestion for revision. (See the following section, "Providing Feedback on Language: When? How?", for more examples.) When possible, it is helpful for students to practice using these tools with a sample assignment and discussing their evaluations before breaking into pairs or small groups.

- **Make opportunities for debriefing.** It is always useful to invite feedback on how peer review went for students and what they have learned for the next draft or next assignment. This feedback can be provided via a short, in-class writing assignment or a writer's memo accompanying the submission of the revised draft.

Providing Feedback on Language: When? How?

One of the questions we are asked most frequently by our faculty colleagues is, When and how should we take language into account in our feedback and evaluation of student writing? This is a complex question as we are often trying to balance two values: accountability and accommodation. That is, we want to help students continue to grow as language users, including through language-focused feedback. At the same time, as we discussed in Chapter 3, we do not want to penalize students for linguistic difference, keeping in mind that "native-like" English is not a reasonable or ethical expectation for most international students who use English as an additional language (e.g., Silva, 1997). In this section, we present some insights and strategies that can help us balance two commitments.

Feedback and Grading Are Different

It is first important to consider whether we need to take language into account at all. For some assignments, we may give feedback on language for the students' benefit (or because they have requested it), but we do not necessarily need to factor grammar, style, or mechanics into the assignment grade, unless that is one of our learning goals for the assignment. If and when we do focus on language in our feedback, we try to focus on linguistic patterns and choices that most impact the clarity and effectiveness of the writing. (See Sidebar 32, Student Perspective on Grammar.)

Language May Not Be the Biggest Issue

We also should keep in mind that if a student's writing is difficult for us to understand and evaluate, "language" may not be the primary reason. Instructors responding to the work of multilingual writers often assume that

> **32**
>
> **Student Perspective on Grammar**
>
> "Making grammar an ungraded component of the rubric would be the most inclusive approach, in my opinion. Instructors should trust their students to use the extra time effectively, and I believe that without the added anxiety [about] grammatical errors, students are more likely to use any extra time effectively."
> —*Student from India*

any concerns in the writing can be traced back to language differences. However, when our expectations for an assignment are unmet, there may be a variety of issues at play: A writer may not have understood the course topic or materials they are writing about, or they might be confused about the genre or goals for the assignment. (This is why some of the scaffolding strategies we laid out earlier in this chapter, as well as in Chapter 3, are so important!)

There may also be academic cultural values at play. As we discussed in Chapter 2, U.S. academic culture tends to value efficiency and directness. It is the scholar's job to make their work clear and easy to navigate. For example, in most genres of academic writing and speaking, students are expected to state their thesis or overview early. In other academic cultures, readers might be expected to figure out the central argument or key points as they go. Most U.S. academic writing also tends to prioritize concision and cohesion in the structure of sentences and paragraphs, rather than sophistication and aesthetics. (See Atkinson, 2003, Connor, 1996, and Shapiro, 2022, for more on links between academic culture and writing conventions.)

In essence, writing or speech that a U.S.-educated instructor (or classmate) considers indirect, disorganized, or rambling might be seen differently in another academic culture. Conversely, work that seems cogent and well organized to an instructor or student raised in the United States may feel "dumbed-down" or even disrespectful to a reader or listener educated in a different academic culture.

Of course, rhetorical norms also differ by genre, audience, and discipline, which may also influence how we respond to student work. A student who is comfortable doing literary analysis, for example, may be surprised to find that a detailed analysis of long passages of text is not common in social science and STEM disciplines.

We bring these points up to remind instructors that when a piece of writing from a multilingual writer does not meet our expectations, there may be more than simply language difference at play. Often, focusing on genre and structure in feedback and revision improves the clarity of the work significantly—whether or not we are attending to grammar, style, or mechanics at the sentence level. This is not to say that feedback on grammar is not helpful at times, however. See Sidebar 33, Providing Feedback on Grammar, and additional points in the following sections for insights that can inform when and how we provide language-focused feedback effectively.

Written Accents (Like Spoken Ones) Are Normal

When it comes to sentence-level language, we often introduce the concept of "written accent" (Harris & Silva, 1993) to our colleagues—and sometimes to students themselves—as a way to determine whether language difference is in fact a hindrance to comprehensibility. Just as we may hear a variety of spoken accents in our classrooms and faculty meetings, we can expect to see a variety of indicators of language difference in student writing, including awkward phrasing, unusual word choice, and unconventional grammar and mechanics. The question is not whether the writing has "differences," but whether those differences actually hinder communication. In other words, from an asset perspective, language variation is not in itself a problem.

This insight is particularly important for instructors who are themselves monolingual English speakers and may not realize that an aspect of English that seems "basic" to them is in fact quite complex! For example, we have had colleagues ask us why a particular student is sometimes misusing articles (*a, an, the*), without realizing that English has a notoriously difficult article system. Moreover, incorrect or missing articles do not usually interfere significantly with the clarity of the work—they are just "odd" to instructors who are not used to multilingual writing.

Clarity—Not "Correctness"—Matters Most

Not all grammatical or stylistic "errors" have the same impact on the clarity of the writing. Articles (*a, an, the*), as noted, rarely have an impact. (In fact, some linguists have suggested only half-jokingly that the primary function of articles in English is to distinguish "native" from "non-native" speakers!) In contrast, verb usage (e.g., subject-verb agreement errors, verb tense inconsistency) creates more confusion for readers because verbs are the "core" of English sentences. (For a list of common grammatical issues and the extent to which they impact clarity, see Appendix D.)

> **Providing Feedback on Grammar**
>
> **Focus on clarity—not native-ness.** Consider whether grammar hinders your ability to understand what the student is trying to say.
>
> **Attend to grammar later in the assignment process.** Deal with grammar after macro-level issues (e.g., content, evidence, organization) have been addressed. Otherwise, students may be more reluctant to make major changes to content.
>
> **Point out errors; don't simply "correct" students' work for them.** If students must make the corrections themselves, they will become more effective self-editors.
>
> **Look for patterns of error, not isolated instances.** See Appendix D for common errors seen in college-level writing.
>
> **Remember what matters most.** The goal is not to see an "error-free" piece of writing; rather, it is to see student learning and growth.

Focusing on comprehensibility rather than "correctness" in student writing can be quite freeing for instructors who have in the past felt pressure to highlight every "error" they observed, no matter what its impact on clarity. We can choose to ignore aspects of the writing that are atypical or unconventional, focusing instead on whether the writing is effective in meeting the student's rhetorical goals. This focus also helps us be more equitable in our grading of student writing so that we are using our evaluation to maximize learning, rather than as a punishment or reward for factors that are outside of students' control, as we discussed in Chapter 3.

Rubrics allow us to signal to students that we are taking clarity into account but are not allowing language, style, and mechanics to "make or break" their grades. In the sample research paper rubric discussed later this chapter, a student could receive a lower grade (10/15) for the criterion "Clarity, conciseness, and word choice" because some portions of the paper were wordy or difficult to follow. But that student could receive a higher grade (28/30) for "Type and use of sources" if they have demonstrated an ability to find and incorporate appropriate secondary sources in the writing. Because the latter is worth twice as much of the paper grade (30 versus 15 points), the overall grade for the assignment would emphasize higher-order concerns, but the student would still receive the message that they should focus on language use as part of the revision for this assignment or the drafting of the next.

If there are sections of the writing that are particularly difficult to follow, making it hard to access the content, we may provide students with an opportunity for selective revision—that is, an opportunity to keep working on targeted aspects of the paper to improve clarity, conciseness, or another aspect of language use. This opportunity will be most successful if we first meet with students to help identify areas where language use is a concern, or if we give them some points to focus on with a writing center tutor.

The key takeaway is that it is not necessary—or ethical, frankly—to make language itself a primary criterion in grading student work (except, perhaps, in a world language course). Research suggests, in fact, that too much emphasis on accuracy (e.g., by correcting every grammatical or mechanical error) can shift students' attention away from other aspects (e.g., argumentation, organization) that usually have a greater impact on the overall effectiveness of their work (e.g., Knoch et al., 2015).

Evaluating Student Work Equitably

As discussed earlier, one equitable assessment strategy is to distinguish between feedback and grading. A grade (for an assignment or for the course) can be based on a variety of criteria that have to do with the product, but it can also take into account students' engagement with the process, which can be an important way of honoring the time, energy, growth, and reflection that struggling students in particular have put into their work.

Rubrics as a Tool for Grading—and Teaching

As we have touched on already, one of the best ways to make grading expectations transparent is to create a rubric for the assignment, which outlines the criteria by which it will be graded and describes the characteristics of each criterion.

International students tend to be particularly appreciative of rubrics for several reasons. First, for students who are completing genres of writing (or other academic work, such as projects) that are less familiar to them, rubrics offer some clarity around expectations. Second, rubrics give students an idea of what they should prioritize in their work, which can lower their anxiety levels and help them with time management. We can even include criteria such as "takes into account global contexts" or "demonstrates intercultural awareness" to make clear that we value some of the particular contributions of multilingual and international students. If we present the grading rubric alongside samples of work from past students, we can make sure everyone is clear about what they need to be doing and how. Finally, rubrics can also help students self-assess their work and set personal goals for improvement throughout the unit or semester.

Developing a rubric can be surprisingly difficult. Many instructors have an intuitive sense of what they are looking for in an A- or B-level paper or project, but they may have a hard time articulating those expectations clearly to students. However, in the process of creating the rubric, instructors usually come away with a clearer sense of their expectations, which allows us to be more transparent with students, as discussed earlier.

One concern instructors sometimes express about rubrics is that such explicit articulations might encourage conformity or stifle student creativity. This concern is particularly prominent among U.S. instructors, given the importance of originality in U.S. academic culture, as discussed in Chapter 2. Research suggests, however, that the benefits of explicit grading criteria far outweigh the potential concerns (Andrade & Heritage, 2017; Brookhart, 2013; Panadero & Jonsson, 2013). Rubrics, checklists, and other resources in fact help inspire (and reassure) students more than they constrain them.

Using a rubric also forces instructors to be clear and consistent when evaluating student work. This is particularly important when grading the work of multilingual writers because (as discussed earlier) the presence of a "written accent" (e.g., Harris & Silva, 1993) can affect our judgment of student work. Most instructors find that the time and energy they invest in creating a rubric is well spent and that grading often takes less time when guided by previously articulated criteria.

There are two types of rubrics commonly used in higher education. A holistic rubric has multiple criteria grouped under a single performance level or grade category. This rubric is useful for small or low-stakes assignments (e.g., homework, reflection journals, or mini-online research tasks) or those in which multiple criteria are not easily disentangled.

An analytic rubric, in contrast, tends to be more useful for work that will be graded according to multiple criteria. This type of rubric includes a description of each criterion that will be scored, as well as a rating scale for each criterion. For example, Figure 4.1 shows the criteria that one author, Shawna, uses to grade the final draft of her students' library research projects in her first-year writing course Language and Social Justice.

Guidelines for Creating Rubrics

Include a variety of criteria. Include criteria such as argumentation, use of sources, organization, tone and word choice, formatting, and clarity or effectiveness of language use, and weight them according to your learning priorities.

Think critically about the ratings. Consider weighing the content criteria more heavily than mechanics, grammar, or speech clarity to avoid penalizing international students.

Explain what each criterion means. For example, "content" might involve responding to the prompt, having an arguable thesis, or using evidence.

Model use of the rubric. Show samples of student work and ask students to rate them using the rubric.

Don't "reinvent the wheel." There are a variety of discipline-specific (and genre-specific) rubrics that can be found online. (There are samples in Appendix B as well.) However, be sure to adapt each rubric to the specific goals of your assignments.

Figure 4.1 *Sample Rubric for a Library Research Paper*

Criterion	Key questions	Points possible
Title, introduction, research question	Is the introduction engaging? Is the research question relevant and explicit?	20
Type and use of sources	Are sources credible or scholarly? Are a variety of strategies used (e.g., paraphrase, quotation, etc.)?	30
Organization and transitions	Is there a sense of progression both between and within paragraphs?	25
Clarity, conciseness, and word choice	Does the writer avoid repetition? Is the writing accessible but academic in tone? Does the writer use a variety of grammatical structures that sound polished?	15
Professionalism	Does the writer use APA style effectively? Is the paper proofread? Was there sufficient attention to mechanics and other details?	10

See Sidebar 34, Guidelines for Creating Rubrics, as well as Appendix B for more sample rubrics for a variety of assignment types.

It is worth noting that the rubric in Figure 4.1 does not have a section for grammar or style specifically, but it does include a criterion called "Clarity, conciseness, and word choice." This intentional choice allows us to hold students accountable for using the appropriate genre, rhetorical, and disciplinary conventions, without penalizing students for having a "written accent," as we discussed earlier.

Many instructors allow students to provide input on the construction of the rubric. This collaborative approach helps students feel more invested in the assessment process and also gives them an opportunity to review and reflect on the course goals. This approach is particularly useful for individualized, interdisciplinary, and multimodal projects, for which it is difficult to create a universal rubric. We can work with students to create a rubric that honors their intentions and fits with our learning goals and expectations.

Rubrics are also helpful for students' self-reflection and personal evaluation of their work. Alongside their submission of work, students may be asked to rate what they have done (process and/or product) against the criteria we have articulated in our rubrics. We can even build on their self-assessment in our feedback and grading of their work, as we will explore further. This approach to assessment not only saves us time but also adds an element of dialogue and collaboration to what often feels like a unidirectional grading process. The short "writer's memo" assignment discussed earlier can be a good starting point for students' self-assessment.

In sum, rubrics send students a message about what is most important in their work, and they are therefore an important tool for teaching and for evaluation. By weighting the elements that matter most—and those that we are teaching most explicitly in our courses—we can "level the playing field" a bit for international students and others who have had less experience with academic writing in U.S. English (e.g., Inoue, 2019; Tomaš & Shapiro, 2021). We can go even further in our commitment to equity and linguistically responsive instruction by grading for process and growth, not just product, as we discuss in the next section.

Factor Labor, Growth, and Reflection Into the Grade

Traditionally, instructors tend to focus most of their grading of student work on the product alone, with the logic that better quality work is a sign of more labor, learning, and growth on the part of the student. However, we know that the quality of student writing correlates strongly with the educational opportunities and resources students had prior to entering our classrooms. Students who had more opportunities to write, receive feedback, and revise in secondary school come into higher education with a "leg up." And of course, those who did so in U.S. English (versus another language or dialect) have an additional benefit that is often unacknowledged. We have all likely worked with students who have been able to produce "A-level" work with a minimal amount of time and energy simply because of the prior training they received.

We can help promote equity for international students—and for domestic students who have not had the same linguistic, educational, and socioeconomic privileges as others—by taking process into account. This approach can take many forms. One is to include criteria in our grading rubrics that are focused on labor and growth, such as the following:

- timely submission of drafts

- completion of scaffolding activities and assignments

- responsiveness to feedback on earlier drafts

- improvement from the previous draft (or from the last assignment)

- reflection on the final product (e.g., via a writer's memo, as discussed earlier)

Going Further With Alternative Grading

Some instructors have advocated for doing away with "product" grades altogether, in favor of what antiracist writing assessment expert Asao Inoue (2019) calls "labor-based assessment." One option is to use grading contracts that evaluate students' effort in the course, rather than providing separate grades on individual assignments (Danielewicz & Elbow, 2009). With this approach, the instructor defines what students must do to achieve a particular grade, with options for raising the grade if they miss a step or assignment. Some instructors ask students to complete learning or labor logs throughout the semester, where they document their time on task and what they are learning.

A related approach is "specifications grading" (Nilson, 2016), which is similar to a "pass/fail" or "satisfactory/unsatisfactory" grade. All students who reach a particular level of proficiency on an assignment receive the same grade, and students are given multiple opportunities and support to reach that level.

These are just some of the ways that instructors in many disciplines are working to put less emphasis on grades and more on student effort and engagement. These approaches are part of a larger movement toward "ungrading," which has been growing significantly in higher education in the United States and abroad (e.g., Blum, 2020; Williams, 2020). Research has found that alternative approaches to grading can improve student motivation, lower student stress, and deepen learning (Khanna, 2015; Morales, 2014). However, some studies have suggested that international students may be resistant at first to these unfamiliar approaches (e.g., Hiller & Hietapelto, 2001; Larson, 2021). For this reason, we need to be *transparent and specific* with students about why we are using these approaches and how the process will work, just as we do with our other pedagogical decisions.

A final option for taking process into account alongside product is to use a portfolio model, in which students choose which work from class to showcase, then reflect on how that work demonstrates their learning and growth. Instructors can provide a grade for the work itself, as well as for the reflection component, which can be oral, written, or multimodal (e.g., Klenowski et al., 2006; Song & August, 2002). Students can share highlights from their portfolios in class or even with the local community.

Gallen (2021) has argued that portfolios are an important piece of social justice pedagogy, as they invite deep and sustained reflection as well as a more equitable means for evaluating learning. Portfolios are also a useful resource that students can adapt for academic and professional purposes in the future (e.g., for graduate school applications). Some instructors (such as Raichle) use electronic portfolios for which students design a simple website on a platform like Google Sites or Wix.

Other Issues to Consider

In this section, we address some of the other topics we are often consulted about when it comes to assignments and assessments.

Supporting Collaborative Work

Many U.S. instructors have at least one major assignment or project for which students are invited or required to collaborate with classmates. When designed and scaffolded appropriately, group projects or assignments can teach students skills for difficult dialogue, creative problem-solving, and effective collaboration. Moreover, as we discussed in Chapter 3, having opportunities to connect frequently with classmates, both during and outside of class, can deepen students' social connections and facilitate a sense of belonging, which can be particularly helpful for international students looking to broaden their social circles. However, many instructors can likely remember experiences with collaboration that were ineffective, stressful, and uneven in terms of workload distribution.

Here are some tips for ensuring that collaborative work is a positive experience for everyone:

- **Start small.** Use in-class collaborations (see Chapter 3 for examples) to help students become comfortable working together.

- **Think carefully about goals and structure.** Consider group size and composition, processes for group formation, and distribution of work. Some instructors use a "mix and mingle" activity that allows group members to learn about each other's strengths, work styles, and preferences before forming groups.

- **Provide a clear rationale for the collaborative work.** Make sure you also give clear instructions, including helping students discuss roles and responsibilities (e.g., How often should the group meet? How might they divide up the workload? What support and opportunities for feedback will we provide along the way?).

- **Conduct frequent check-ins.** These check-ins can allow individual students to share how the process is going. As much as possible, give students time in class to connect with their group members. This may be followed by a brief debrief with the larger group.

- **Help students stay organized.** For instance, you can suggest technological tools (e.g., Google Drive) that can help them keep track of documents and resources and require scaffolding assignments (See Chapter 3 for more on instructional scaffolding.)

- **Give students an opportunity to provide feedback on each group member's work and on their overall experience.** For example, Raichle's students complete an online form in which they evaluate each group member's contributions and effectiveness with communication, as well as their own.

Plagiarism or Unconventional Source Use

We are often asked by colleagues about ways to address plagiarism in the classroom. Those who would like an extended discussion of this topic are invited to read Zuzana and Shawna's recent article "From Crisis to Opportunity: Turning Questions About 'Plagiarism' Into Conversations About Linguistically Responsive Pedagogy" (Tomaš & Shapiro, 2021). To read the full article, visit the companion website for this book (www.tesol.org/FISS). In this section, we discuss a few highlights.

Instructors need to focus on proactively teaching source use as a skill rather than simply expecting appropriate source use as a given. The more energy we invest in highlighting the role of secondary sources in our assignments and providing strategies and models for effective source use, the better our students will become at using sources appropriately in their work. Spending even a bit of time in class on the question "How do I find, evaluate, and incorporate sources into this assignment?" can have an enormous payoff for students—and can save us valuable time and energy that might otherwise be spent trying to deal with cases of suspected plagiarism (Mott-Smith et al., 2017; Tomaš & Shapiro, 2021). In other words, focusing on pedagogy means instructors spend less time and energy thinking about punishment.

Here are some other strategies that can help us address this difficult topic proactively:

- Invest time in scaffolding assignments, including opportunities for frequent check-ins and feedback (i.e., the strategies outlined earlier in this chapter) around source use. These assignments can include reading logs, annotated bibliographies, outlines that include citations, and sharing sessions during class. Having these small assignments due helps keep students on track with finding, digesting, and using sources.

- Keep in mind that understandings of intellectual property and textual ownership or borrowing differ by academic culture and may be unfamiliar to students with less experience in U.S. education systems (see Chapter 2 for more on this topic). In some academic cultures (and in some literary writing in English), using recognized words from a well-respected authority without explicit attribution is a sign of rhetorical sophistication. This strategy is read as demonstrating respect and cleverness, rather than dishonesty.

- Remember that source use is a linguistically demanding skill set that can be particularly challenging for multilingual writers, who may struggle to process, paraphrase, and cite ideas from secondary sources. Students learning this skill set may sometimes produce "patchwriting" (Howard, 1995) that too closely mirrors the original text. Rather than seeing this as the result of dishonesty, we should consider it a developmental step and an indicator that students need more instruction and practice.

- When you encounter an instance of suspected plagiarism, try not to make hasty judgments about a student's intention. Often, plagiarism is the result of disorganization and time scarcity, rather than an intent to deceive (Pecorari & Petric, 2014; Walker, 2010). This does not excuse the behavior, of course, but it may inform how we approach the conversation.

- Take time for your own emotional processing. Encountering inappropriate source use—especially when we have built in the appropriate scaffolding and other support—might cause you to feel angry, offended, or even personally betrayed (Benesch, 2018).

When addressing suspected plagiarism with students, it is helpful to focus the conversation around student learning rather than punishment. We can ease into a conversation about the situation by saying, "I'd like to talk with you about strategies for using secondary sources in your work," rather than "You've committed plagiarism in this assignment."

The aforementioned *TESOL Quarterly* article (Tomaš & Shapiro, 2021) elaborates on all of these points, helping instructors think about writing from sources in a comprehensive way. The article also includes a link with several additional resources, including practical books on this topic (e.g., Mott-Smith et al., 2017) and multimedia that can be used outside the classroom to support international student understanding of this important topic.

Special Accommodations

Some of our colleagues have asked us whether additional accommodations might be justified to "level the playing field" for international students. Of course, some students may already receive mandatory accommodations because of documented disabilities—although research suggests that international students are often underrepresented in this regard (e.g., Owen, 2020; we discuss this topic more in Chapter 5). However, there are additional steps we can take to increase students' likelihood of success with our assignments and other assessments. Ideally, these are accommodations we offer to all students, as part of a Universal or Inclusive Design approach (e.g., CAST, 2018; Collier, 2020).

Translation support. One helpful accommodation to minimize linguistic barriers is to allow students to access a translation application on their phones or bring a bilingual dictionary to the exam. We can also invite students to ask clarifying questions after they have had a chance to review the exam, which may allow them to clarify essential vocabulary.

Additional time on exams. As we discussed earlier, completing academic work in an additional language simply takes longer. For this reason, some instructors offer extra time for students who request it, allowing those students to arrive early or stay longer to complete the exam. Some campuses even have a staffed office where students can go to complete a proctored or supervised exam. Of course, many domestic students would also benefit from having additional time, especially if they have challenges with information processing. So making this option available to everyone is the best approach, in terms of inclusivity and access. It is also important to ensure that we have allotted sufficient time for taking the exam in the first place, as many instructors underestimate how long an exam will take the average student.

Extensions on assignments. International students may also benefit from extensions on assignments, particularly if they want to take advantage of support from writing and learning centers. Again, making this accommodation available to all students is best, though one caution we have is that extensions should be specific and short term. When given an unlimited amount of time to submit much of their course work, students may become overwhelmed, when multiple deadlines converge at the end of the semester. Many students struggle with perfectionism—including many international students (e.g., Wei et al., 2007)—and having a firm but fair deadline is helpful for forcing them to finish and submit an assignment, even if it is less than "perfect."

Early feedback. One way we can minimize last-minute requests for extensions is to invite students to submit a draft of an assignment for feedback *before* the assignment deadline. We often make this offer to all of our students and find that only a few actually take advantage of it. We sometimes give a nudge to those we know have been struggling, with a comment or an email where we say, "I'd really love to see where you're at with this assignment before it's due. Let's make a time to meet, or you can send me what you have by [date]." When students do submit an early draft, there is payoff on both ends: We receive a better submission in the end, and the students feel more confident about their work. (See Sidebar 35, Student Perspective on Feedback.)

Opportunities to retake tests or rewrite assignments. We occasionally allow students to retake part or all of a quiz or exam or to redo an assignment, especially if it becomes clear that they misread the question or prompt or misunderstood the requirements. As with other suggestions, this option should ideally be made available to any student. If we allow this option, it is crucial to ask students to reflect on what went wrong the first time so they can do better in the future. Was time management the issue or gaps in knowledge or skills? Are struggles with mental health or social or cultural adjustment playing a role? (See Chapter 5 for more on helping students find support beyond what we offer in the classroom.)

Alternative assignments. Occasionally, our colleagues will ask us whether they should create a separate assignment for students who are struggling significantly to keep up with the demands of a course. These sorts of decisions can only be made on a case-by-case basis. Generally, though, we prefer to provide multiple assessment options for *all* students to choose from, rather than making a separate assignment for a subgroup of students. Weimer (2013), for example, provides students with a "cafeteria of assignment options" (p. 5) from which to choose. A shy student might choose to write a paper rather than give an oral presentation. One who struggles with test anxiety may opt to take weekly quizzes instead of longer midterm and final exams. If choice in assignments is not possible, we find that it is better to provide additional scaffolding (see Chapter 3) rather than changing assignment expectations.

Conclusion: Toward Empowerment and Advocacy

We hope this chapter has offered useful insights into how to use assignments and assessments to facilitate and measure student learning. Some of our suggestions may require rethinking approaches to assignment design, feedback, and evaluation, as well as to exams and other forms of assessment. We wish to remind readers that the ultimate goal of this "rethinking" is not to lower our academic standards but to create the conditions by which students can show us their learning and growth in meeting those high standards. Some assessment experts call this "bias for best" (Swain, 1983; see also Fox, 2004). When students feel empowered to learn, and to demonstrate their learning, they feel a greater sense of belonging in our classrooms. In Chapter 5, we will discuss other ways to help empower and advocate for international students in our classrooms and on our campuses. We will also consider additional ways to recognize and build on the cultural, linguistic, and other assets that international students bring to our institutions.

CHAPTER 5

Supporting the Whole Student Across the Institution

Throughout this book, we have discussed how internationalization presents both opportunities and challenges in higher education. We have offered strategies instructors can use to support international students through some of the cultural, linguistic, and other academic challenges they may face in our classrooms, with a focus on increasing access and recognizing student assets. In this chapter, we lean in even more to the "opportunities" side of the equation. We also consider additional ways to increase students' agency in achieving their academic, professional, and personal goals, both in and outside of the classroom. Drawing on Shapiro et al. (2016), we define *agency* as a student's capacity for making informed decisions, with an awareness of constraints and consequences. These decisions can include everything from their selection of academic courses and programs of study to their participation in extracurricular activities to the linguistic and rhetorical choices they make in their coursework. Our job as instructors is to identify opportunities for decision-making and help students gain the information and skills they need to make those decisions confidently. We can also work more broadly at our institutions to create more "optimal conditions" (Shapiro et al., 2016, p. 33) that maximize students' opportunities for this sort of decision-making.

Making informed decisions is part of a larger skill set that has been gaining increased attention in higher education in recent years: social and emotional learning (SEL). Although SEL has been more prominent in scholarship focused on primary and secondary education, it has made its way into much of the educational literature on postsecondary contexts as well (e.g., Seal et al., 2010). Research has found that SEL capacities, which include relationship-building with oneself and others, can help improve educational access and outcomes. This means that SEL is a core component of diversity, equity, inclusion, and access (DEIA) and antiracism work (Collaborative for Academic, Social, and Emotional Learning, n.d.; Madden-Dent, 2021; Yeh et al., 2022). This chapter aims to tie these

36

Reflection Questions About International Students

1. What do you see as the greatest benefits of having international students in your classes? At your institution?

2. Have you witnessed or heard about any concerns related to institutional alienation or discrimination against international students?

3. What do you do to help international students feel welcome and included in your classes?

4. What is your program or institution doing well to support international students? What could it do better?

37

Responding to Deficit Conceptions of International Students

Following are examples of comments we have heard from faculty and administrators about international students for whom English is an additional language. How might you respond to a colleague who expressed one of these concerns?

"Many [international students] lack very basic skills that we assume they have when they get to our class. Consequently, they have to work much harder than the rest of the class, and even then they have a hard time succeeding."
—Instructor in communication studies

"Many of our students who fail in the very large intro series are ESL [English as a second language] students. Staff limitations prevent our department from dedicating additional resources to help [these] students."
—Instructor in biology

"Stricter prerequisites for entry into the university, and into certain classes, would help students whose language skills still need remediation to receive that attention instead of failing classes."
—Instructor in engineering

often-disparate conversations (SEL and DEIA) together by reiterating and expanding on our suggestions for supporting the "whole student" in the classroom and across the institution.

Many of us also have opportunities to do institutional work beyond our classrooms through our institutional service, administration, and faculty development. As we take part in these institution-wide activities, we can advocate for fair policies, welcoming campuses, and inclusive teaching practices for international students. Moreover, we can help amplify student voices, ensuring that international students' needs, assets, and experiences are not left out of campus-wide conversations, as is often the case with institutional DEIA and antiracism initiatives (Koo et al., 2021; Lee, 2007; Tavares, 2021a; Wick & Willis, 2020). To explain why our role as advocates is so important, it is helpful to discuss the ethical considerations that play into the recruitment of international students, which sometimes lead to inaccurate assumptions and unfair treatment. (See Sidebar 36, Reflection Questions About International Students.)

Ethical Considerations

As discussed in Chapter 1, international student recruitment is often driven by financial incentives, with little planning to ensure the success of students at the institution (e.g., Singh, 2021). Thus, administrators may be inclined to view international students primarily as a revenue source, losing sight of their responsibilities to this student population. Instructors, in turn, may accuse administrators or admissions staff of bringing students to campus who were unprepared for academic work (see Sidebar 37, Responding to Deficit Conceptions of International Students). Lost in this "blame game" are the students themselves, who come to our institutions with rich and varied goals, needs, and assets.

Fair Treatment and Inclusion of International Students

Although instructors may have little say in admissions policies and strategic planning processes, they can think deeply about how international students are treated in their own programs and departments. They can also amplify student voices when concerns arise. Indeed, a number of cross-institutional studies have indicated that international students often experience discrimination or unfair treatment at institutions of higher education (e.g., Australia Human Rights Commission, 2012; Equality and Human Rights Commission [UK], 2019; New Zealand Ministry of Education, 2008). Although the U.S. government has yet to take up this line of research, concerns about the treatment of international students have been raised by many U.S.-based scholars (e.g., Lee, 2010; Sherry et al., 2010; Tummala-Narra & Claudius, 2013), and some governmental entities have pledged a commitment to promoting a positive experience for international students (NSW Government, 2012; U.S. Department of State & U.S. Department of Education, 2021).

These reports raise a number of difficult questions, such as the following:

- What are the rights of international students, in terms of institutional policies, resources, and support?

- Whose responsibility is it to ensure that these rights are respected?

- How can we work together to ensure that international students are included in institutional conversations about diversity, equity, inclusion, and belonging?

At the core of these questions are the goals of inclusion and equity. As Bittencourt et al. (2021) argue, rather than expecting international students to change so they can succeed at our institutions, our institutions need to change to make sure international students feel welcomed, valued, and supported. In the following sections, we review pedagogical strategies and institutional resources that can play a role in promoting inclusion for international students. We then look more closely at how instructors and institutions can recognize and tap into the assets of international students and their contributions to the larger academic community.

Supporting Social and Emotional Adjustment

Research has found that a variety of factors contribute to students' adjustment and sense of inclusion at institutions. Academic factors such as the range of course offerings, availability of support, and classroom climate play a major role in helping students feel that they belong (or do not belong) at our institutions. Social factors such as the availability of cocurricular and extracurricular opportunities and opportunities to build social connections also play an important role (Bender et al., 2019; Rienties et al., 2012; Zhang & Goodson, 2011).

For international students in particular, social and academic experiences are often mutually reinforcing (Freeman & Li, 2019; Seithers et al., 2022). Struggle in one area often leads to difficulty in the other, creating a vicious cycle: For example, international students often report high levels of loneliness and homesickness during their initial adjustment period, and these feelings may be sustained for a longer amount of time than is typical for domestic students (Andrade, 2006; Poyrazli & Lopez, 2007). These feelings may be exacerbated by the fact that academic coursework often occupies such a large amount of student time, as discussed in Chapter 3, that students may feel they must put their social lives on hold in order to achieve academic success.

38

Student Perspective on Social Connections

"There seems to be an added responsibility on the part of the international students to make an effort to branch out their social connections, without recognition of the same for domestic students. . . . All students have to leave their comfort zones . . . to create an inclusive environment conducive for social connections."
—International student from India

When they do find time and energy for social interaction, international students may find it difficult to connect with domestic peers (Andrade, 2006; Bittencourt et al., 2021; Chen & Yeung, 2019; also see Sidebar 38, Student Perspective on Social Connections). They may find it easier to spend most of their social time with peers from similar linguistic and cultural backgrounds, which can lead to low overall satisfaction with their study abroad experience (Misra et al., 2003; Rienties et al., 2012; Zhang & Goodson, 2011). Additionally, research suggests that building social connections with members of the host community can offer some protection from the harmful effects of language discrimination, as well as depression and anxiety (Sun et al., 2021; Wei et al., 2012).

The good news for instructors is that there is much we can do to promote students' social and emotional well-being alongside their learning of academic content. We already do so by putting into practice many of the pedagogical strategies discussed throughout this book. For example, students feel less stressed and overwhelmed in classes where the instructor has articulated clear goals and expectations, integrated scaffolding into instruction and assignments, and designed fair and effective feedback and assessment practices—all points discussed at length in Chapters 2, 3, and 4. Previous chapters have also included strategies for promoting interaction among students, both during and outside of class, which can help students build and strengthen their social connections (Cena et al., 2021; Seithers et al., 2022; Shu et al., 2020). Thus, by implementing pedagogical "best practices," we not only facilitate student learning but also help promote students' sense of belonging and agency at our institutions (Freeman & Li, 2019; Shapiro, 2020). In the sections that follow, we delve further into other strategies that can help promote social and emotional adjustment.

Community-Building in the Classroom

Although we touched on community-building in Chapters 2 and 3, we are returning to it here as a strategy for promoting social connections. Many instructors find that if they take the time to get to know their international students (or any students, for that matter) early in the semester, they develop a rapport, which makes it more likely that students will reach out if and when they begin to struggle academically or socially. Here are some ways we can learn more about students early in the semester:

39

Jigsaw Survey

Following are questions from a jigsaw survey activity used in an interdisciplinary first-year seminar on the "American dream" that included many international students.

- What characteristics or values do you commonly associate with Americans and/or the United States?

- What words and/or images come to mind when you think of the "American dream"?

- Our college town is what many would call a "classic" American small town. What were your first impressions of the town? Did it seem classically "American" to you?

- Do you think the United States is truly unique compared with other countries? How (or why not)?

- How do you think the "American dream" is perceived in other parts of the world, and what contributes to those perceptions?

- Facilitate icebreakers that are designed to not only promote social connections but also pique students' interest in course content. One first-day activity we have found to be particularly effective in achieving these goals is a jigsaw survey, in which each student (or pair of students) is assigned a particular question, which students use to conduct short interviews with their classmates. They then report back on their findings, orally or in writing. (See Sidebar 39, Jigsaw Survey, for an example and Chapter 2 for more classroom activities that help build community.)

- Require short, one-on-one (or small-group) meetings with students early in the semester. As we discussed in Chapter 2, many international students are intimidated by the thought of approaching the instructor once they are struggling in the course. Holding brief, low-stakes meetings (10–15 minutes) early on helps decrease students' anxiety about visiting the instructor's office later and reinforces the message that instructors are available to help students when they need it. For larger classes, you may wish to have students visit in pairs or small groups. Some instructors rotate through the class to conduct short (5-minute) "mini-meetings" with each student while others are working on a task or assignment.

- Assign a short writing assignment that allows students to share their background with the course content and disclose relevant personal information, if they so choose. Examples include a 1- to 2-page reflection paper, a questionnaire, or a post to the class discussion board. Here are some questions one might ask in this initial assignment:

  - Why have you chosen to take this course?

  - What do you hope to learn?

  - What background experiences (including other coursework) have you had related to this topic?

  - What else might be helpful for me to know about you, such as your educational background or preferred learning styles?

- Ask questions in class discussions or assignments that invite students to draw on their personal backgrounds. Keep in mind that many international students do not want to feel forced to disclose but do appreciate the opportunity to share information they feel is most relevant. Usually, they prefer to disclose this information privately (e.g., in writing) or at least with advanced warning, rather than through cold-calling. We have all worked with students who felt alienated because they were "spotlighted" for being "foreign" or "ESL" (English as a second language). It is best to take an inclusive approach that draws on the background experiences of

40

Spotlighting: An Example and Some Alternatives

Example: A student from Ecuador was extremely offended when her professor announced in class that "all ESL students should meet with a writing tutor before handing in their papers." She was also bothered that the professor sometimes called on her in class discussions to represent the Latin American perspective.

Why might the student have felt alienated by these experiences? What could the instructor have done differently?

To avoid putting international students "on the spot," consider asking more inclusive questions:

Rather than asking only international students ...

- Where are you from?

- Are you a nonnative speaker of English?

- What do people in your country think about this issue?

Instead, ask all students ...

- Where did you grow up or attend high school?-

- Where do you feel like a "local"? (See Taiye Selasi's 2014 TED Talk, "Don't Ask me Where I'm From, Ask Me Where I'm a Local.")

- How has your background influenced your response to our class material?

- What perspectives might be missing from our discussion thus far?

all students—not just those who are from other countries (see Sidebar 40, Spotlighting: An Example and Some Alternatives).

Facilitating Peer-to-Peer Interaction

We can also promote social adjustment and inclusion by encouraging meaningful interaction in the classroom. We have discussed some of these points in earlier chapters, but we are revisiting them here to remind instructors that these sorts of interactions increase students' social integration as well as their academic learning.

In addition to icebreakers and other "get to know you" activities, we can use low-stakes group activities—such as small-group discussion, group problem-solving or other application tasks, and peer feedback—to strengthen social ties. More sustained group projects can encourage social interaction as well, but these must be well designed with clear goals, defined student roles, and relevant scaffolding. Otherwise, group projects can in fact exacerbate feelings of alienation for international students, rather than integration (Leki, 2001; Seithers et al., 2022). Chapters 3 and 4 offer additional suggestions for facilitating group activities and assignments.

Online platforms and social media can also be used to encourage peer-to-peer interaction outside regular class hours. Many students appreciate having a class email list or group chat. Some instructors also make use of a class website, blog, or course management system (e.g., Moodle, Blackboard, or Instructure) that becomes a place to post course materials, extend class discussions, answer questions, and promote conversation.

Advising and Mentoring International Students

Many of us have relationships with international students beyond their work in our classes. If we serve as advisers, mentors, or supervisors for international students, it can be helpful to take into account several factors.

Educational history and goals. We can learn more about students' past schooling experiences by asking questions such as the following:

- Have you studied at an English-dominant institution already, or is this your first time doing academic coursework in English (outside of a language course)?

- What are your academic and professional goals in the short term and long term?

- What factors led you to choose this institution, this major or program of study, etc.?

- Whose influence weighs on you most in your academic decision-making? How do you take their influence into account without losing sight of your own goals and interests?

Academic strengths and challenges. It can be helpful to talk through students' perceptions of their strengths and challenges. International students who are struggling are particularly appreciative of insights that help them figure out whether their challenges are connected to language background or cultural background knowledge or whether they are inherent to a particular course, project, or program of study. Note that areas of concern may vary widely depending on the level and academic discipline: Students in science, technology, engineering, and mathematics (STEM) may have concerns about collaborative work or exams, while graduate students in humanities courses may be more focused on writing theses or articles or preparing to work as teaching assistants.

Visa restrictions. International students may have visa requirements that limit their access to certain types of employment, as well as to internships, study abroad, and other opportunities. They may hope to remain in the United States after graduation for Optional Practical Training (OPT), but this is only available to students in certain fields of study. (See Appendix F for more information about international student visa policies in the United States).

Funding issues. Some international students have grants or scholarships that come with certain expectations (e.g., that they must study or major in a particular academic discipline, that they participate in particular activities). Students may also have expenses or financial obligations that influence their decisions around employment and other opportunities. It is important to keep in mind as well that many of the financial aid options available to domestic students (e.g., Pell Grants, federally subsidized loans) are not offered to international students.

Encouraging Students to Ask for Help

As discussed earlier and in Chapter 2, international students may struggle with when and how to seek help from instructors (Owen, 2020). There are a number of reasons for this (see Sidebar 41, What Prevents Students From Seeking Help?). Often, the moment when they most need our help is the same moment when they are too overwhelmed or even ashamed to ask.

We can normalize and encourage proactive help-seeking in several ways.

- Provide explicit information on anticipated workload in the course syllabus, answering questions such as the following:
  - How many hours should students plan to devote to out-of-class work, such as readings, assignments, group work, and test preparation?

41

What Prevents Students From Seeking Help?

This is one of the questions we are asked most often by our colleagues. Although we have offered insights on this question at several points in this volume, here is a quick summary:

- **Understandings of the teacher-student relationship differ across academic cultures.** Students may have been taught that asking for individual help from a teacher is inappropriate, as it implies that the instructor is not doing their job effectively (see more on this Chapter 2).

- **Students feel embarrassed.** It is not uncommon for international students to think they are the only person in class who is struggling, even if this is not the case. For example, a Korean student who was doing poorly on exams in her biochemistry course told one of us, "Most of my friends are native speakers, so they don't have such problems." This was untrue—in fact, the exams in this department were known to be difficult, and the department had begun to offer review sessions and study groups to help all students prepare, but the student was unaware of these resources.

- **Students are intimidated.** It can be both intellectually and emotionally overwhelming to talk with an instructor individually about one's academic or other struggles. It is even more challenging for students who use English as an additional language.

- **Students may be punishing themselves.** It is worth noting that students sometimes admit that they avoid reaching out to us because they feel guilty or ashamed for not being in touch sooner. In other words, they may feel that it is "too late" or that they "don't deserve" to have our support.

A good rule of thumb is that students should plan to spend at least 2 to 3 hours of out-of-class time for every hour of class.

- How much reading is expected per week, on average, and how thoroughly are students expected to have done the readings? If the readings are lengthy, or there are multiple pieces, what should students prioritize? (See Chapter 3 for more on supporting students with assigned readings and media.)

- Are there peak times in the course when students will need to devote additional time, or is the workload steady throughout the term? (We can also promote strategies and resources for time management, including through learning centers or other offices, as discussed later this chapter.)

• State directly in the syllabus and in class what office hours are for, and remind students often that they are encouraged to stop by simply to chat, even if they do not have a major question or problem. Here are additional ways to encourage students to meet with us:

- Reserve the last few minutes of class, or a window of time after class, for students who have questions. (Many feel more comfortable talking to an instructor in the classroom or another public space than visiting a private office.)

- Create online or in-class sign-ups for meeting appointments. (We have used Doodle, Calendly, and MeetMe, as well as Google Sheets, for scheduling).

- Allow students to visit in pairs or small groups.

• Check in with students at multiple points in the semester to see how class is going for them and whether they have any concerns. This can be done with a 5- to 10-minute free-write at the end of class or through an online survey.

• Reach out directly to students who are struggling or missing class, via email or a private conversation after class (away from other students), and encourage them to make an appointment for a longer conversation. Try to use friendly, caring, and clear language in these emails (see the example in Sidebar 42, Checking in With Students via Email).

• Offer optional workshops for a subset of students who might need them. These could take place outside of class time or could be offered at the end of class so that students who do not need the additional skills or support can leave early. It can be helpful to partner with writing or learning center staff, librarians, or other colleagues to develop these workshops (more on this in subsequent sections). Although these workshops take time to prepare and facilitate, they often save us time when we respond to and evaluate student work.

42

Checking in With Students via Email

Below is a typical email we might send to a student who has missed multiple class sessions or who did not turn in one or more major assignments. Note the use of friendly but directive language.

Subject line: Checking in

Dear [student name],

We missed seeing you in class today. I wanted to check in to see how you're doing, since you also missed a class last week. Please let me know how things are going. I'd also love to find a time to talk to make sure you get caught up. Are you free during my office hours from 3–4 p.m. tomorrow? I have other times available on Friday, too—you can sign up online at [URL].

I look forward to hearing from you,

Prof. [Name]

- Remind students often of the many other forms of support available to them, recognizing that in times of overwhelm, it may take longer for the information and encouragement to sink in.

Promoting Other Support Resources

Most institutions have a variety of programs and resources designed for academic, social, and psychological support, including (in many cases) particular offices or programs dedicated to international students. This section reviews some of the resources we can remind students are part of the support system available to them. Some of these resources are less common at universities in other countries, so our reminders to international students can be helpful.

It is important that we frame these resources as a complement to—rather than a replacement for—the support we ourselves offer to students. We point this out because we occasionally hear from international students who approached their instructor about a concern and were immediately directed elsewhere. Sometimes before they talk about "solutions," students appreciate an opportunity to process with us what they are struggling with and what they need. Even if we cannot "fix" the issue, we can offer a listening ear and make sure students feel we care about them. Within that caring conversation, we can also recommend other resources that would help. It is also important to remember that most of the resources discussed here can be helpful to *all students*—not just international students. Thus, in keeping with a Universal Design approach (mentioned in Chapter 1), we should share these resources with the entire class by listing them in our course syllabi, on websites, or via other resources.

International Student Offices

Most institutions have an office or program devoted to international students, and these may also include support for international faculty and staff. The role of the international student office varies with each institution. At a minimum, staff in these offices assist international students and scholars with visa paperwork and other legal and financial issues, which are often quite complex. Some offices continue to work with alumni, who may qualify to remain in the host country for up to 3 years for OPT. All U.S. institutions that admit international students are required to have a Designated School Official who ensures that the institutions are in compliance with laws and policies outlined by the Student and Exchange Visitor Program. (See Appendix F for more information on student visas, test scores, and other international and exchange student policies.)

Most international student offices also provide some form of orientation or other programming for new arrivals, as well as supplemental academic advising. Moreover, they may offer cocurricular and extracurricular programming to support cultural adjustment and foster intercultural exchange among students. Staff in these offices can also help to promote offerings from other campus entities, such as

- academic skills workshops;

- language-focused social events (e.g., English conversation groups, international coffee hour, and language exchanges with U.S. students who are learning a world language);
- field trips and community service opportunities; and
- partnerships with host families in the local community (e.g., to share meals; celebrate holidays; and receive occasional assistance with transportation, storage, or other needs).

Finally, staff in these offices can answer questions we have about intercultural communication, student support, visa issues, and other topics. We have found our own international student office colleagues to be an incredible resource for our students—and for us! A final point to keep in mind is that some institutions include students who are undocumented immigrants (e.g., students who are covered by the Deferred Action for Childhood Arrivals program, known as DACA) in their lists of "non-U.S. citizens." They may offer support for this subset of students on issues such as tax forms, visa processing, and other areas of concern. However, support for DACA students is not usually a primary function of those offices. Another excellent source of information and support around these issues is the Association of International Educators, also known as NAFSA (www.nafsa.org).

Financial Aid Offices

As noted earlier, some international students may struggle to cover costs associated with studying abroad, even if they receive financial aid from their country of origin or from the host institution. Students often encounter costs they had not anticipated, such as

- winter clothing (or other seasonally appropriate clothing);
- textbooks and office supplies;
- fees for field trips, lab sessions, or other experiential learning; and
- travel and visa costs.

Moreover, international students may be averse to taking out loans—particularly since low-interest loans may only be available to domestic students. Financial aid offices can help international students explore what aid they qualify for and what on-campus job opportunities might be a good fit, especially because many international students are not allowed to seek other forms of employment.

Writing Centers

Research has found that international students tend to make use of writing centers more frequently than their domestic counterparts (e.g., Hall, 2013). We see this as a positive trend, as it reveals that these students are proactively seeking support and receiving feedback on their work, as well as engaging in social interaction with a caring peer or staff member. Students who are encouraged or required to visit the writing center in their first semester often return in future semesters (Gordon, 2008).

One point to keep in mind about writing centers, however, is that peer tutors are *not* editors or proofreaders. They are encouraged to focus on content and organizational issues before looking at language. Much of the tutoring session may be spent talking about ideas and writing processes, rather than "correcting" student writing. This can create a mismatch between what international students are looking for (or have been told by an instructor to get help with) and what the tutors are prepared to do. Although many centers do train tutors to address language-related issues (e.g., Bruce & Rafoth, 2009), most centers are still committed to a dialogic approach rather than a didactic one. In essence, before sending a student to the writing center, we need to understand the center's goals, expectations, and procedures.

One exciting development in writing centers in recent years has been a shift toward a multilingual model, which often includes more intentional recruitment of writing tutors who are multilingual and multidialectal, as well as an expansion of offerings to include support for writing in languages other than English (e.g., Rafoth, 2015). This shift means that international students may be in demand not just as clients of the writing center but as staff, too! Indeed, all three of us (the authors) have mentored international students who worked in writing centers and were a tremendous asset.

Learning Centers

Many institutions have learning centers that can offer support in other academic areas besides writing, such as academic reading, oral presentations, or mathematics and quantitative skills. In addition to individual tutoring, some learning centers offer support through workshops, course-specific study groups, and other programming. These centers sometimes have professional staff who can work directly with a class to teach particular skills, such as time management or use of instructional technology.

Staff members in writing and learning centers often enjoy partnering with instructors to provide targeted resources or to scaffold larger assignments. For example, time management coaches at some institutions will meet with students individually to map out a weekly schedule that includes time for coursework, as well as meals, sleep, exercise, and other commitments. Learning centers may offer particular support for graduate students, such as writing groups or practice sessions for those preparing to give high-stakes oral presentations. As is the case with writing centers, it is helpful to consult with staff at the learning center about what they have to offer and how they approach their work.

Many institutions have centers for teaching and learning that not only provide support to students but also offer faculty development opportunities for instructors and teaching assistants. Many of the suggestions and resources we have shared in this book, in fact, came out of our conversations and workshops with colleagues on our campuses, in sessions offered through the centers at our institutions.

Library Support

Library research can be particularly challenging for international students, as it involves not only extensive reading but also the evaluation and synthesis of multiple sources. Library staff often know of the latest tools to help students find, organize, and cite materials appropriately in their papers. These staff can offer support through research workshops or by working with individuals or small groups on their research projects. Instructors can make students aware of these opportunities by mentioning library offerings in the syllabus and, if possible, inviting a librarian to visit class for a workshop or a quick meet-and-greet. At many institutions, librarians are invited to facilitate for-credit workshops or even teach entire courses dedicated to information literacy, data analysis, or other areas of expertise.

English Language Programs

Many institutions offer English language courses for students who are struggling with the linguistic demands of the curriculum. Sometimes these courses are required as part of a conditional admissions program. In other cases, they are optional and may or may not carry academic credit. Many students find these courses to be an excellent complement to their regular academic coursework. English language programs often maintain lists of online resources and sometimes offer cocurricular opportunities for students seeking to build conversational English or improve grammatical accuracy in their writing.

We should be cautious, however, about recommending that a student take an additional English language course, as many students experience this sort of recommendation as stigmatizing. Most of our international students have performed well in past English language classes, and they often have submitted English proficiency test scores to be admitted to the institution. An increasing number of international students also studied abroad successfully as part of their secondary schooling (e.g., Zhang-Wu, 2021). For these reasons, international students may be resistant to the suggestion that their English is "not good enough." Research does in fact suggest that international students, in most cases, benefit more from academic support within the context of their programs of study than from taking additional courses in English as an additional language (Phakiti et al., 2013; Zhang-Wu, 2021). If a student is struggling and we think language proficiency is part of the problem, we can offer a range of options, including strategies and resources particular to our course.

Valuing International Students as an Asset

Supporting students through academic, social, and cultural adjustment processes is an essential piece to the puzzle of increasing students' agency and sense of belonging at our institutions. Another piece to the puzzle is greater awareness of what international students bring to our classrooms and campuses—the assets they can contribute to institutional diversity and global citizenship. In this section, we outline a number of ways instructors can tap into students' cultural and linguistic assets, echoing and building on what we have discussed in previous chapters. See Sidebar 43, International Students as an Asset, for some firsthand perspectives on what international students bring to our classrooms and institutions.

Global and Cross-Cultural Perspectives

Research has found that many instructors appreciate international students who offer new or underrepresented perspectives on course material (Andrade, 2006; Jin & Schneider, 2019; Trice, 2003). In an arts or humanities course, a student who grew up outside the United States might offer an alternative reading of a primary source, or they could bring in an additional philosophical or historical tradition. In social science courses or STEM courses, they might offer insights about how a particular social or ethical issue is viewed in another part of the world or how research methods and priorities vary according to geographic context. These sorts of global and cross-cultural perspectives enrich the classroom experience for everyone.

However, contributions of this kind do not always happen spontaneously. They are much more likely to occur if instructors create space for them through carefully selected course materials, discussion prompts, and assignments. As we do this, the goal is not to put a particular student "on the spot" as the stand-in for an entire country, region, or cultural group (see Sidebar 40, Spotlighting: An Example and Some Alternatives). Rather, we try to invite all students to draw on their background knowledge and lived experiences. Here are some in-class activities that we use for this purpose:

- **Small-group discussion.** Often, students who are hesitant to speak with the large group are much more comfortable sharing in smaller groups—especially if we want them to share about their identities and experiences. We can tailor the questions for small groups to make space for a variety of viewpoints. Another structure that works well for this is think-pair-share, in which students first reflect individually, then share ideas with a partner before addressing the larger group. (This activity is discussed in further detail in Chapters 2 and 3.)

- **Debate/role-play.** As we discussed in Chapter 2, one of the aspects of U.S. culture that many international students find difficult is the emphasis placed on personal opinions and argumentation. Our students (both international and domestic) sometimes ask us, "How are we supposed to have an opinion about something we just began studying a month ago?" One way to engage multiple perspectives while students are still formulating their own views on an issue is to use role-play activities, in which they express a position that may or may not be their own. These activities encourage critical thinking and intellectual flexibility and also help lower anxiety for many international students (Shapiro & Leopold, 2012). Role-play can take a number of forms:

43

International Students as an Asset

"A lot of my students have never been outside their hometown, so it's a benefit for them to be exposed to somebody with different perspectives."
—*Instructor in communications*

"One of my sociology professors has asked me once if I could create a short presentation about how marriage and divorce are perceived in my culture. . . . I was so proud to do this! I felt like I had something to teach others about another way."
—*Student from Chile*

"International students [in our program] have been real leaders in several student organizations and greatly contributed to our university life."
—*Administrator in the office of international student support*

"On occasion, I work with international students who want to extend on connections between the countries and institutions that they came from and the host institution. One helped me set up an international study abroad in her small town!"
—*Instructor in TESOL and education*

One option is an in-class roundtable or panel conversation, in which students represent a particular author or perspective (having prepared ahead of time, if possible). Another option is to assign a written role-play, such as an imagined letter exchange, dialogue, or social media exchange between individuals with divergent views (see Shapiro, 2022, for more examples of oral and written role-play).

- **Jigsaw survey.** This activity (which we discussed in Sidebar 39, Jigsaw Survey) can be used throughout the semester to encourage students to share multiple perspectives and gather feedback from their peers on complex or controversial issues.

Some assignments that encourage multiple perspectives include the following:

- **Response papers.** These are a low-stakes way to see whether students understand the readings and to encourage students to draw on their personal backgrounds.

- **Literature review or annotated bibliography.** Students compile a review or bibliography of existing research on a topic that intentionally includes a variety of points of view on that topic. Giving students the opportunity to include sources in languages other than English or from scholars outside the United States is another way to invite diverse perspectives!

- **Primary research projects.** Students survey or interview their classmates to gain a more in-depth perspective on controversial or global issues. They can present their findings orally, in writing, or in a multimodal format, such as a poster, Prezi, or Padlet. We usually allow students to conduct the survey or interview in whatever language is most comfortable to the participant, which is another gesture toward linguistic inclusion.

- **Student-led discussion.** When students are given the opportunity to generate discussion questions or to serve as moderators, they may feel more comfortable introducing additional viewpoints into the conversation. Facilitating discussion also builds students' confidence and leadership skills.

- **Online discussion boards.** Because many international students feel most confident when they have a chance to write and review their contributions ahead of time, they often become the most active participants in online discussion—particularly asynchronous discussion (where students have multiple hours or days to post their responses). Given how today's students interact with technology, it is important to select app-based spaces that allow engagement via smartphones. For example, many students prefer Discord Servers, Slack Channels, and Padlet boards over forums in a learning management system like Canvas.

We want to make two final notes on including global and cross-cultural perspectives in your class. First, remember that students themselves are an excellent source of feedback and insight into how to diversify the global and cultural perspectives in our courses. We can explicitly invite their suggestions as part of their regular feedback to us. Some instructors include a question like the following on their institutional course evaluation forms: "What suggestions do you have for broadening the range of perspectives and issues presented in this course?"

The second note is that thinking about "global" aspects of our courses does not mean we leave behind local contexts and concerns. Instead, we aim to link global to local. Some scholars use the term *glocal* to highlight this important linkage (e.g., Patel & Lynch, 2013). Community engagement opportunities, which we discuss later in this chapter, are one excellent way to help students make these connections.

Linguistic Diversity, Inclusion, and Equity

There has been a great deal of discussion among scholars in recent years about the importance of language as part of DEIA within the U.S. education system (e.g., Baker-Bell, 2020; Clements & Petray, 2021; Hudley et al., 2022). Although these conversations have often focused heavily on multidialectal students, such as those who use Black/African American English, they also pertain to international students who use English as an additional language or are most comfortable with non-U.S. varieties of English (e.g., Schreiber et al., 2021). Instructors' judgments of students' capabilities—and their evaluation of student work—are often informed by a sense that language difference is a problem, rather than a resource (Canagarajah, 2006; Losey & Shuck, 2021; Matsuda, 2006).

Instructors can promote a more positive orientation to linguistic diversity—one that recognizes the value of multilingualism at individual and societal levels. We know that language is inherently connected to race and other aspects of social identity (Flores & Rosa, 2015; García & Wei, 2014b). Research has also found that multilingualism offers a number of cognitive benefits, including improved mental processing speed, executive functioning capacities, and multitasking abilities (Bialystok, 2010). Knowledge of another language also builds *metalinguistic awareness*—consciousness about the role language plays in our lives and in the world, which is crucial for any student who wishes to engage effectively in a globally interconnected world (e.g., Abe & Shapiro, 2021). This awareness can help increase our understanding of how language is linked to identity, privilege, and power as well, what some scholars call *critical language awareness* (e.g., Alim, 2005; Shapiro, 2022).

Here are some ways that we can treat linguistic diversity as a resource in our curriculum.

Language as a lens for social analysis. In many humanities and social science courses, themes such as race, class, gender, and nationality constitute the dominant analytical framework. One theme that some instructors have added to this list is language. By looking at issues of privilege and power as they relate to language, students can develop a deeper understanding of the issue at hand. We have encountered instructors using language as a lens through which to examine immigration policy, environmental activism, mental health, gender bias in STEM, racial prejudice in the U.S. judicial system, and many other pressing issues (see Shapiro, 2022, for more on this topic).

Discipline-specific language. In almost every discipline, there is a line of scholarship focusing on the ways that language is used to shape and convey academic values and priorities. This is the focus of much of the research in English for Specific Purposes and Writing in the Disciplines. By talking about the norms and conventions in writing (and speech) within our fields of study, we help increase students' understanding about academic disciplines as discourse communities (Duff, 2010; Shapiro, 2022). This in turn can increase students' sense of membership and belonging within those communities (Lillis & Harrington, 2015). For example, we can talk about how the use of passive voice (versus active voice) verbs in the Methods section of an empirical study has traditionally been seen as the best way to convey objectivity in research. We can also talk about how many scientific journals, such as *Nature*, have begun to encourage more use of first-person "I," as a way to make the writing more accessible (e.g., Ellerton, 2020).

Language as content. Instructors who have a high degree of autonomy in the content of their courses can promote linguistic inclusion by incorporating linguistic topics into their course design. Here is a sampling of themes that we have seen in interdisciplinary academic writing courses: language and identity, language and the brain, cross-cultural communication, issues in translation (e.g., of literary texts), linguistic discrimination and language rights, inclusive language, political discourse, and critical media analysis.

One specific topic that many international students enjoy working with is World Englishes. Learning about the many dialects (varieties) of English around the world offers students an opportunity to share from personal experience and to engage with scholarship in a variety of disciplines (e.g., linguistics, history, world literature, political science). Such a course can also explore critical questions such as these:

- What factors led to English's dominance as a global language?

- Who benefits from, and who might be harmed by, this dominance?

- What skills do today's global citizens need in order to communicate effectively with English speakers around the world?

- What is the ethical responsibility of English language educators worldwide to sustain non-English home languages and cultures?

For more on international student responses to World Englishes content, see Sidebar 44, Student Perspectives on World Englishes, as well as Shapiro (2022) and Shapiro et al. (2016).

Examining linguistic prejudice. Incorporating language-related topics into our courses also offers opportunities to explore social justice issues, including linguistic prejudice. Research has found that *linguistic profiling*—that is, unfair perceptions and treatment of an individual or group based on assumptions about their speech or writing—is pervasive in many sectors of U.S. society and can create barriers to employment, housing, and educational opportunities (Baugh, 2018; Lippi-Green, 2012). Within our own institutions, students and faculty who use English as an additional language are often judged as being less intelligent or capable than native English speakers (e.g., Fan et al., 2019; Lee & Du, 2020; Lindsey & Crusan, 2011). This can impact how student contributions to class discussion are received, as well as how their work is evaluated—and even whether they are successful in their applications for awards or other opportunities!

By taking language into account in discussing issues of justice and equity in the curriculum, we offer insights that might make our institutions more linguistically inclusive. Indeed, a number of scholars have called for more attention to linguistic justice in our classrooms and across our campuses (e.g., Baker-Bell, 2020; Clements & Petray, 2021; Hudley et al., 2022). This includes recognizing how our assumptions about language are informed by racism and other implicit biases (Flores & Rosa, 2015).

One starting place for countering linguistic biases is to remind students (and colleagues) that all of us can build up our skill sets for understanding a variety of spoken accents and writing styles. In other words, rather than expecting "accent reduction" on the part of those for whom English is an additional language (or dialect), we can increase our own capacities for "accent recognition" (Warner et al., 2021). This skill for working across language difference is in fact a valuable professional and civic skill set as our communities and workplaces become increasingly diverse and globalized.

Translingual/plurilingual approaches. Another way to demonstrate that we value language difference is to create space for a wider range of linguistic resources within our curricula through a translingual or plurilingual approach (e.g., Brinkschulte et al., 2018; Horner & Tetrault, 2017; Losey & Shuck, 2021). One way to do this is to broaden the range of language backgrounds represented in our course materials, perhaps by including texts or media from users of a wide range of World Englishes, as noted earlier. Another option is to craft assignments that allow students themselves to incorporate a variety of languages, dialects, or styles. Research suggests, in fact, that this sort of language mixing, which many scholars call *translanguaging* (e.g., García et al., 2017; García & Wei, 2014a), is common within multilingual and multidialectal communities, and making space for this practice in the classroom can increase students' agency as language users. Although not every assignment is well suited to inviting translanguaging, we have seen public writing, creative writing, and other projects that incorporate this practice in courses in a wide range of disciplines. (See Sidebar 45, Examples of Translingualism.)

> **45**
>
> **Examples of Translingualism**
>
> *Here are three sample activities that use a translingual approach:*
>
> - Analyze an author's use of different "codes"—such as multiple languages or dialects or shifts from a more formal to an informal style. When is this most rhetorically effective?
>
> - Notice uses of translanguaging or code-mixing by politicians, celebrities, and other public figures. The NPR podcast *Code Switch* discusses this topic frequently (www.npr.org/sections/codeswitch).
>
> - Discuss when it might be appropriate for students to incorporate multiple codes in their own writing. What are the potential benefits? What are the risks?

Beyond the Classroom

There are a number of ways instructors and institutions can support international student agency beyond the classroom as well.

Service learning/community engagement. Engaging with the local community not only broadens international students' perspectives on their host country but also allows them to give back and feel a greater sense of belonging. We have seen particularly high representation among international students in certain community service endeavors, such as alternative spring break trips and youth mentoring programs. (It is essential to confirm eligibility, of course, because a student's nonimmigrant status may limit eligibility for certain kinds of travel.)

Research assistantships. International students often appreciate the opportunity to work more closely with a faculty member on research. We have had international students join us in institutional research projects that have informed the writing of this book, in fact. For example, students might interview other international students about their experiences at the institution or interview instructors about their work with other international students.

Tutoring. Many institutions make a special effort to recruit international students as tutors or study group leaders. This opportunity allows students to display their knowledge of a particular content area or a world language that is the focus of study for their peers.

Student mentoring. Many international students who are juniors and seniors enjoy serving as mentors for new arrivals, helping their peers navigate the process of cultural adjustment. International students can also help U.S. students prepare for their own study abroad experiences in other countries.

Student clubs. Many institutions have organizations that are targeted to particular ethnic groups. While these are certainly important, many international students are equally interested in groups that allow them to make closer connections with U.S. students. Clubs focused on international development, global politics, sports, cross-cultural exchange, and other international issues are particularly effective in this regard. (See Sidebar 46, Integrative Student Organizations.)

Special events. We have attended a number of events that were arranged by a combination of U.S. and international students and showcased the talents, interests, and knowledge of both groups. Some of our favorite examples include

- a talent show featuring dance, music, and other work, performed by a mix of domestic and international students;

46

Integrative Student Organizations

Following are descriptions of three student organizations that encourage interaction between U.S. and international students.

- **International cooking club.** International students can teach their peers how to cook popular dishes from their home countries. This can coincide with important holidays, such as Lunar New Year or Eid al-Fitr.

- **GlobeMed.** This organization has chapters on many U.S. campuses and focuses on health equity in impoverished communities (www.globemed.org).

- **Multilingual magazines.** Some institutions have publication opportunities for multilingual and multidialectal students, such as essays and creative writing that use multiple languages or dialects, translation projects, and even multimodal projects.

- a panel discussion entitled "Uncovering the Veil," which included both Muslim international students and Muslim American students expressing a variety of perspectives on the hijab (traditional head covering); and

- an international research symposium featuring U.S.-focused projects from international students as well as globally oriented projects from U.S. students who had returned recently from study abroad.

Engaging in Institution-Wide Advocacy

As we conclude our discussion of supporting international student agency, it is important to consider how we as instructors can advocate for and with students—particularly if we have administrative roles or engage in institutional service. Given the ethical issues raised at the start of this chapter, we can seek out opportunities to elevate and amplify student voices to ensure that international students are treated equitably. One way to be an advocate is to explicitly counter stereotypes and deficit narratives about international students. When we hear colleagues make generalizations or quick assumptions about students' socioeconomic backgrounds, English levels, academic preparation, and so on, we can counter these points—perhaps even using information from this book!

We can also encourage—and even facilitate—institution-wide conversations about international student experiences, supports, and assets. As instructors, we often have a perspective that may be lacking among admissions staff or administrators because we see what happens to students *after they arrive* at our institutions. In other words, we can help create a feedback loop that can inform policies, resource allocation, and other institutional decision-making. Here are eight steps institutions can take—maybe with some advocacy on our part—to ensure they are inclusive and equitable toward international students:

1. Collect and analyze data about international students to learn more about language backgrounds, educational experience prior to college, patterns of coursework (e.g., departments and programs with the highest percentages of international students), and academic achievement (e.g., areas of academic struggle, representation of international student in departmental honors, awards, and leadership opportunities).

2. Gather feedback systematically from international students about their academic, cocurricular, and social experiences at the institution, using surveys, focus groups, or interviews. This may reveal concerns that were not on our radar. For example, at Shawna's institution, international students expressed concerns about the limited internship opportunities available to non-U.S. citizens. Once administrators were aware of this concern, the corresponding office began to pursue more international internships. Feedback from students can also help us ensure that our support resources are tailored to the needs of particular subgroups (e.g., undergraduate versus graduate students, international teaching assistants, etc.).

3. Establish an interdepartmental committee or task force to discuss internationalization efforts, if such a committee does not already exist. Such a committee should include representatives from admissions, financial aid, the international student office, and the diversity or DEI office, as well as faculty, staff, and student representatives from various departments and programs.

4. Make sure that other institutional DEIA initiatives do not overlook the needs and assets of international students and instructors. As we touched on earlier, conversations about DEIA often focus more on domestic students, despite the fact that many of the issues the initiatives aim to address, such as systemic racism, also have a significant impact on international students (Tavares, 2021a).

5. Advocate for asset-oriented policies and practices, such as credit-bearing language and writing support courses, training for writing and learning center staff in supporting multilingual students, and a curriculum that invites global and cross-cultural perspectives across disciplines, as discussed earlier. We can also make sure that international students are represented on advisory committees, in student government, and in other institutional decision-making processes.

6. Prioritize giving international students clear and timely information about academic opportunities and performance. This information can include midterm academic progress reports or warning systems so that any student who is struggling will receive feedback—and be made aware of options and resources—before the end of the semester.

7. Offer more professional development opportunities for faculty and staff, focusing on supporting and including students from diverse cultural and linguistic backgrounds. Such opportunities can be created in collaboration with specialists in TESOL and applied linguistics, Writing Across the Curriculum, and inclusive or antiracist pedagogy. Where possible, provide incentives (e.g., stipends) for facilitators and participants. Administrators at some institutions have even used part or all of the previous edition of this book as the primary reading for workshops and seminars focused on international student support! (Note that this edition includes a reading guide in the Afterword.)

8. Remember to include international faculty and staff in these conversations and initiatives. These faculty and staff may offer valuable insights into institutional adjustment and global and cross-cultural curricula. They may also have particular needs, such as writing or oral communication support, assistance with tax forms and other paperwork, and culturally responsive health care or other services.

It can also be inspiring for international students to have opportunities to talk with international faculty and staff. An economics professor from Argentina visited one of our writing classes once to talk about her experience as a multilingual scholar. She inspired confidence by telling students, "I love my 'foreign' accent! It's a beautiful part of me—like freckles or a birthmark!"

For more on this positive orientation to accents, check out George Mason University's Written Accents project (https://writtenaccents.gmu.edu/).

Conclusion: Toward Global Citizenship for All

The increase in international students in U.S. higher education presents an opportunity for institutions to think deeply and critically about their goals for all students. If one of those goals is global citizenship, then it is crucial that we work collectively to ensure that all students—international and domestic—feel welcomed, included, and supported. We can do this through the content and facilitation of our courses, as well as through our institutional support and advocacy work. By continuing to reflect on the needs and strengths of international students, instructors in U.S. higher education can lead the way in furthering the goals of equity, inclusion, and internationalization at their institutions. In the Afterword and appendixes that follow this chapter, we synthesize some of the key insights from this text and provide additional resources to support instructors in their work with international students.

Afterword

In closing this book, we wish to remind readers that attending more closely to the experiences, goals, and assets of international students can have a transformative impact on our classrooms and institutions. This impact can extend into our own intellectual lives, as well as into our communities. As feminist scholar and activist bell hooks (1994, p. 34) explains in her book *Teaching to Transgress*,

> All of us in the academy and in the culture as a whole are called to renew our minds if we are to transform educational institutions—and society—so that the way we live, teach, and work can reflect our joy in cultural diversity, our passion for justice, and our love of freedom.

This sort of transformation happens slowly, however, and requires sustained reflection and action. There are no quick fixes. Indeed, part of the process is recognizing that a mindset of "fixing" students can itself be a barrier to equity and inclusion. We hope the insights and strategies in this book have provided fodder for instructors who are committed to the difficult but rewarding work of valuing and supporting international students across the curriculum.

To support our readers in enacting this commitment, we have created two new resources for this second edition. The first is our Top 10 Impactful Strategies list, which includes key strategies that have been shared throughout this book and can inform multiple aspects of instruction, including curriculum design, materials selection, classroom interaction, assignment creation and scaffolding, and feedback and assessment. We hope this list serves as a helpful reference tool for readers who want to recall some of the most impactful steps they can take in their pedagogical practice to increase access and value the assets of international students.

The second resource is the Reading Guide, which provides key questions pertaining to each chapter. These questions are designed to orient readers to some of the most important points from the text and to inform pedagogical reflection and decision-making. They may also be useful for readers who wish to facilitate professional learning with their colleagues or administrators around one or more chapters of this book. As a reminder, there are additional materials contained in the appendixes and e-resources for this book.

Top 10 Impactful Strategies

1. Use a **Backward Design** approach, starting with your desired outcomes, then deciding on the means of assessing those outcomes in ways that are inclusive of diverse student populations. Then design curricula and instruction to build up to those outcomes and assessments.

2. Make **community-building** a primary focus throughout the term—not just in the first week. Incorporate opportunities for students to connect early and often. Reach out proactively to students who are in danger of falling behind.

3. Be **transparent and explicit** about your expectations for student behavior, including how to communicate best with you and with each other, what "class participation" entails, and when and how to seek additional support. Use tools such as rubrics and checklists to remind students of these expectations, and create friendly opportunities for clarification.

4. When it comes to language use in student work, shift your expectation away from "native-like" proficiency and toward students' ability to convey their learning effectively (i.e., **"clarity," rather than "correctness"**).

5. Use **instructional scaffolding** to support students in achieving high expectations. This can include teaching strategies for reading and exam preparation, using graphic organizers (and other visuals) to aid comprehension, and incorporating formative assessment to gauge student learning.

6. Promote **peer-to-peer interaction** during and outside of class in a variety of groupings and formats (e.g., pairs, small groups, online discussion, etc.). Explain to students why discussion and collaboration are crucial to their learning.

7. Find ways to **recognize and tap into the assets** that international students bring to our classes, including global perspectives, multilingual competence, and intercultural awareness. Make space for these assets within course materials, during class discussions, and in student work.

8. Invite frequent **feedback and self-reflection** from students to promote their long-term learning and growth and to understand their barriers and challenges. Remember that there are many ways to gather this input—orally, in writing, during or outside of class, and so on.

9. Aim to promote linguistic, cultural, and global awareness **among all students**, rather than targeting international students.

10. Consider how international students might be more **intentionally included in institutional diversity, equity, inclusion, and access** (DEIA) and antiracism initiatives. Consider how to collaborate with academic support entities at your institution (e.g., librarians, writing and learning centers, etc.) rather than "outsourcing" student support.

Reading Guide

Chapter 1: Introduction

1. What do you know about the international students on your campus and in your program or department? What would you like to learn?

2. What challenges and opportunities often come up in faculty and administrator conversations about international students at your institution and in your particular department or program?

3. What are you already doing in your classroom and curriculum that you know is supportive of international students?

Chapter 2: Supporting Cultural Adjustment and Inclusion

1. Which of the academic cultural values discussed in this chapter do you see most prominently in your program or department (e.g., individualism, informality, efficiency, directness)?

2. Are there other features of the academic culture at your institution that often come as a surprise to international students?

3. What are some expectations or norms that you could be more transparent or explicit about with students?

4. What do you already do to build community in and around your classroom and institution? What would you like to do more of to build community?

5. How do you promote interaction among students in your classes? Is there anything new you'd like to try?

6. What have you done—or could you do—to broaden the cultural and global perspectives that are included in your course design and assignments?

Chapter 3: Supporting Language Development With Linguistically Inclusive Pedagogy

1. What have you experienced as a language learner, and how might your past experience influence the ways you see and support international students for whom English is an additional language?

2. When you are working with a student who is struggling, how might you determine whether language proficiency is a factor (versus other things like academic culture, as discussed in Chapter 2)?

    c. If language proficiency is a factor, what kinds of scaffolding or resources might you use to support students with the linguistic challenges of your course?

3. How does the insight that "native-like" proficiency in English is usually an unrealistic goal change the way you teach—and perhaps how you evaluate student work as well?

4. What are some ways you use scaffolding, interaction, and noticing in your own courses? (See the graphic organizer on p. 44.)

5. What are some additional ideas from this chapter you would like to try?

6. How might you—and your students—become more adept at communicating across language difference?

Chapter 4: Effective and Equitable Assignments and Assessments

1. What summative assessments do you use most in your courses?

2. What strategies do you use for formative assessment—and are there ways to do this more in your classes?

3. How clear and specific are your assignment and assessment instructions? Where might they be improved? (E.g., see the list of criteria on pp. 68–69.)

4. Where might you increase your scaffolding, feedback, or other support for assignments and assessments?

5. How effective—and efficient—are your current feedback practices? Are there changes you could make, based on the insights in this chapter, that might benefit students *and* ensure you're investing your time and energy wisely?

6. How do you decide whether and when to give language-specific feedback on your course assignments? Does this chapter change how you think about language-specific feedback?

7. What other suggestions from this chapter (regarding feedback, grading and evaluation, accommodations, etc.) do you already use—or could you start using—to help promote equity in your classes?

Chapter 5: Supporting the Whole Student

1. To what extent were you already familiar with the ethical concerns discussed early in the chapter? Have you observed any of the deficit perspectives (p. 90) at your own institution?

2. What do you already do to build community and strengthen relationships with and among students? Are there new ideas you'd like to try?

3. What are some ways that you show you value what international students bring to our courses and institutions? Are there additional ways you might draw on their linguistic resources, cultural backgrounds, or global perspectives?

4. Which of the eight institution-wide steps (pp. 107–108) are already happening at your institution? What additional steps might be most beneficial? Who might you reach out to in order to engage institution-wide conversations about international student support?

Conclusion

We hope that both of these resources—and the book as a whole—have strengthened your sense of agency in working with international students. We invite you to reach out to us to share your own stories, strategies, resources, and challenges by completing the contact form on the companion website for this book (www.tesol.org/FISS).

References

Abe, S., & Shapiro, S. (2021). Sociolinguistics as a pathway to global citizenship: Critically observing "self" and "other." *Language Awareness*, 30(4), 355–370. https://doi.org/10.1080/09658416.2021.1925289

Adichie, C. N. (2009). *The danger of a single story* [Video]. TED Conferences. https://www.ted.com/talks/chimamanda_ngozi_adichie_the_danger_of_a_single_story

Aktas, F., Pitts, K., Richards, J. C., & Silova, I. (2017). Institutionalizing global citizenship: A critical analysis of higher education programs and curricula. *Journal of Studies in International Education*, 21(1), 65–80. https://doi.org/10.1177/1028315316669815

Alim, H. S. (2005). Critical language awareness in the United States: Revisiting issues and revising pedagogies in a resegregated society. *Educational Researcher*, 34(7), 24–31. https://doi.org/10.3102/0013189X034007024

Amin, N. (1997). Race and the identity of the nonnative ESL teacher. *TESOL Quarterly*, 31(3), 580–583. https://doi.org/10.2307/3587841

Anderson, T. (2015). Seeking internationalization: The state of Canadian higher education. *Canadian Journal of Higher Education*, 45(4), 166–187. https://doi.org/10.47678/cjhe.v45i4.184690

Andrade, H., & Heritage, M. (2017). *Using assessment to enhance learning, achievement, and academic self-regulation*. Routledge.

Andrade, M. S. (2006). International students in English-speaking universities: Adjustment factors. *Journal of Research in International Education*, 5, 131–154. https://doi.org/10.1177/1475240906065589

Anson, C. (1989). Response styles and ways of knowing. In C. Anson (Ed.), *Writing and response: Theory, practice, and research* (pp. 332–366). National Council of Teachers of English.

Arday, J., Belluigi, D. Z., & Thomas, D. (2021). Attempting to break the chain: Reimaging inclusive pedagogy and decolonising the curriculum within the academy. *Educational Philosophy and Theory*, 53(3), 298–313. https://doi.org/10.1080/00131857.2020.1773257

Atkinson, D. (2003). Writing and culture in the post-process era. *Journal of Second Language Writing*, 12(1), 49–63. https://doi.org/10.1016/S1060-3743(02)00126-1

Australia Human Rights Commission. (2012). *Principles to promote and protect the human rights of international students*. https://humanrights.gov.au/sites/default/files/document/publication/international_students_principles.pdf

Avdi, E. (2011). IELTS as a predictor of academic achievement in a master's program. *English Australia Journal*, 26(2), 42–49. https://holmesglen.intersearch.com.au/holmesglencrisjspui/handle/20.500.11800/80

Baker-Bell, A. (2020). *Linguistic justice: Black language, literacy, identity, and pedagogy*. Routledge.

Baugh, J. (2018). *Linguistics in pursuit of justice*. Cambridge University Press.

Bellah, R. N., Madsen, R., Sullivan, W. M., Swidler, A., & Tipton, S. M. (2007). *Habits of the heart: Individualism and commitment in American life* (3rd ed.). University of California Press.

Bender, M., van Osch, Y., Sleegers, W., & Ye, M. (2019). Social support benefits psychological adjustment of international students: Evidence from a meta-analysis. *Journal of Cross-Cultural Psychology*, 50(7), 827–847. https://doi.org/10.1177/0022022119861151

Benesch, S. (2018). Emotions as agency: Feeling rules, emotion labor, and English language teachers' decision-making. *System (Linköping)*, 79, 60–69. https://doi.org/10.1016/j.system.2018.03.015

Bialystok, E. (2010, January 21). *Lifelong bilingualism: Linguistic costs, cognitive benefits, and long-term consequences* [Lecture audio recording]. National Institutes of Health Behavioral and Social Sciences Research Lecture Series. https://videocast.nih.gov/watch=8463

Birdsong, D. (2006). Age and second language acquisition and processing: A selective overview. *Language Learning*, 56, 9–49. https://doi.org/10.1111/j.1467-9922.2006.00353.x

Bittencourt, T., Johnstone, C., Adjei, M., & Seithers, L. (2021). "We see the world different now": Remapping assumptions about international student adaptation. *Journal of Studies in International Education, 25*(1), 35–50. https://doi .org/10.1177/1028315319861366

Bligh, D. A. (2000). *What's the use of lectures?* Jossey-Bass.

Blok, S., Lockwood, R. B., & Frendo, E. (2020). *The 6 principles for exemplary teaching of English learners: Academic and other specific purposes.* TESOL Press.

Blum, S. D. (Ed.). (2020). *Ungrading: Why rating students undermines learning (and what to do instead).* West Virginia University Press.

Brinkschulte, M., Grieshammer, E., & Stoian, M. E. (2018). Translingual academic writing at internationalised universities: Learning from scholars. *Journal of Academic Writing, 8*(2), 150–160. https://doi.org/10.18552/joaw.v8i2.460

Brookhart, S. M. (2013). *How to create and use rubrics for formative assessment and grading.* ASCD.

Bruce, S., & Rafoth, B. (Eds). (2009). *ESL writers: A guide for writing center tutors* (2nd ed.). Boynton/Cook.

Bruner, J. (1985). Child's talk: Learning to use language. *Child Language Teaching and Therapy, 1*(1), 111–114. https://doi .org/10.1177/026565908500100113

Brunsting, N. C., Zachry, C., & Takeuchi, R. (2018). Predictors of undergraduate international student psychosocial adjustment to US universities: A systematic review from 2009–2018. *International Journal of Intercultural Relations, 66*, 22–33. https://doi.org/10.1016/j.ijintrel.2018.06.002

Bryan, C., & Clegg, K. (Eds.). (2019). *Innovative assessment in higher education: A handbook for academic practitioners.* Routledge.

Buckner, E. (2019). The internationalization of higher education: National interpretations of a global model. *Comparative Education Review, 63*(3), 315–336. https://doi.org/10.1086/703794

Buckner, E., Clerk, S., Marroquin, A., & Zhang, Y. (2020). Strategic benefits, symbolic commitments: How Canadian colleges and universities frame internationalization. *Canadian Journal of Higher Education/ Revue canadienne d'enseignement supérieur, 50*(4), 20–36. https://doi.org/10.47678/cjhe .vi0.188827

Burton, V. T., & Ede, L. (Producers), & Robertson, W. (Director). (2005). *Writing across borders.* [Video file]. Oregon State University Writing Center. https://writingcenter.oregonstate.edu/WAB

Canadian Government. (2019). *Building on success: International education strategy (2019-2024).* https://www.international .gc.ca/education/strategy-2019-2024-strategie .aspx?lang=eng

Canagarajah, A. S. (2006). Toward a writing pedagogy of shuttling between languages: Learning from multilingual writers. *College English, 68*(6), 589–604. https://doi.org/ 10.2307/25472177

Carroll, J., & Ryan, J. (Eds). (2005). *Teaching international students: Improving learning for all.* Routledge.

Cassady, J. C. & Johnson, R. E. (2002). Cognitive test anxiety and academic performance. *Contemporary Educational Psychology, 27*(2), 270–295.

CAST. (2018). *Universal Design for Learning Guidelines version 2.2.* http://udlguidelines .cast.org

Cena, E., Burns, S., & Wilson, P. (2021). Sense of belonging and the intercultural and academic experiences among international students at a university in Northern Ireland. *Journal of International Students, 11*(4), 812–831. https://doi.org/10.32674/jis.v11i4.2541

Chaudhury, S. R. (2011). The lecture. *New Directions for Teaching and Learning, 128*, 13–20. https://doi.org/10.1002/tl.464

Chen, J. A., & Yeung, T. S. (2019). Intercultural communication challenges and how professionals can help. In P. Burak (Ed.), *Addressing mental health issues affecting international students* (pp. 71–75). NAFSA.

Childress, L. K. (2009). Internationalization plans for higher education institutions. *Journal of Studies in International Education, 13*(3), 289–309. https://doi.org/10.1177/1028315308329804

Cho, Y., & Bridgeman, B. (2012). Relationship of TOEFL iBT® scores to academic performance: Some evidence from American universities. *Language Testing, 29*(3), 421–442. https://doi .org/10.1177/0265532211430368

Choi, L. J. (2016). Revisiting the issue of native speakerism: "I don't want to speak like a native speaker of English." Language and Education, *30*(1), 72–85. https://doi.org/10.1080/09500782 .2015.1089887

Choudaha, R. (2020). The "China reset" for international undergraduate enrollment. *International Higher Education (101)*. https://ejournals.bc.edu/index.php/ihe/article/view/14277

Clements, G., & Petray, M. J. (Eds.). (2021). *Linguistic discrimination in U.S. higher education: Power, prejudice, impacts, and remedies*. Routledge.

Collaborative for Academic, Social, and Emotional Learning. (n.d.). *Fundamentals of SEL*. https://casel.org/fundamentals-of-sel

Collier, A. (2020, October 26). Inclusive design and design justice: Strategies to shape our classes and communities. *EDUCAUSE Review*. https://er.educause.edu/articles/2020/10/inclusive-design-and-design-justice-strategies-to-shape-our-classes-and-communities

Collier, V. P. (1989). How long? A synthesis of research on academic achievement in second language. *TESOL Quarterly*, *23*(3), 509–531. https://doi.org/10.2307/3586923

Connor, U. (1996). *Contrastive rhetoric: Cross-cultural aspects of second-language writing*. Cambridge University Press.

Cooper, A. Z., & Richards, J. B. (2016). Lectures for adult learners: Breaking old habits in graduate medical education. *Alliance for Academic Internal Medicine*, *130*(3), 376–381. https://doi.org/10.1016/j.amjmed.2016.11.009

Crose, B. (2011). Internationalization of the higher education classroom: Strategies to facilitate intercultural learning and academic success. *International Journal of Teaching and Learning in Higher Education*, *23*(3), 388–395. https://files.eric.ed.gov/fulltext/EJ946165.pdf

Danielewicz, J., & Elbow, P. (2009). A unilateral grading contract to improve learning and teaching. *College Composition and Communication*, 244–268. https://www.jstor.org/stable/40593442

Darvin, R. (2020). Creativity and criticality: Reimagining narratives through translanguaging and transmediation. *Applied Linguistics Review*, *11*(4), 581–606. https://doi.org/10.1515/applirev-2018-0119

Darvin, R., & Norton, B. (2021). Investment and motivation in language learning: What's the difference? *Language Teaching*, 1–12. http://dx.doi.org/10.1017/S0261444821000057

DeKeyser, R. (2013). Age effects in second language learning: Stepping stones toward better understanding. *Language Learning*, *63*(1), 52–67. https://doi.org/10.1111/j.1467-9922.2012.00737.x

Dewaele, J. M., & Furnham, A. (1999). Extraversion: The unloved variable in applied linguistic research. *Language Learning*, *49*(3), 509–544. https://doi.org/10.1111/0023-8333.00098

Dolas, F., Jessner, U., & Cedden, G. (2022). Cognitive advantages of multilingual learning on metalinguistic awareness, working memory and L1 lexicon size: Reconceptualization of linguistic giftedness from a DMM perspective. *Journal of Cognition*, *5*(1), 10. http://doi.org/10.5334/joc.201

Dörnyei, Z. (1990). Conceptualizing motivation in foreign-language learning. *Language Learning*, *40*(1), 45–78. https://doi.org/10.1111/j.1467-1770.1990.tb00954.x

Dörnyei, Z. (2005). *The psychology of the language learner: Individual differences in second language acquisition*. Routledge.

Dovchin, S. (2020). The psychological damages of linguistic racism and international students in Australia. *International Journal of Bilingual Education and Bilingualism*, *23*(7), 804–818. https://doi.org/10.1080/13670050.2020.1759504

Duff, P. A. (2010). Language socialization into academic discourse communities. *Annual Review of Applied Linguistics*, *30*, 169–192. https://doi.org/10.1017/S0267190510000048

Ehrman, M. (1999). Ego boundaries and tolerance of ambiguity in second language learning. In J. Arnold (Ed.), *Affect in language learning* (pp. 68–86). Cambridge University Press.

Ellerton, P. (2020, March 4). We should use "I" more in academic writing—there is benefit to first-person perspective. *The Conversation*. https://theconversation.com/we-should-use-i-more-in-academic-writing-there-is-benefit-to-first-person-perspective-131898

Equality and Human Rights Commission. (2019). *Tackling racial harassment: Universities challenged*. Equality and Human Rights Commission. https://www.equalityhumanrights.com/sites/default/files/tackling-racial-harassment-universities-challenged.pdf

Fan, Y., Shepherd, L. J., Slavich, E., Waters, D., Stone, M., Abel, R., & Johnston, E. L. (2019). Gender and cultural bias in student evaluations: Why representation matters. *PLOS One, 14*(2), e0209749. https://doi.org/10.1371/journal.pone.0209749

Ferris, D. R. (1995). Student reactions to teacher response in multiple-draft composition classrooms. *TESOL Quarterly, 29*(1), 33–53. https://doi.org/10.2307/3587804

Fink, L. D. (2003). *Creating significant learning experiences: An integrated approach to designing college courses.* Jossey-Bass.

Flores, N., & Rosa, J. (2015). Undoing appropriateness: Raciolinguistic ideologies and language diversity in education. *Harvard Educational Review, 85*(2), 149–171. https://doi.org/10.17763/0017-8055.85.2.149

Fox, J. (2004). Biasing for the best in language testing and learning: An interview with Merrill Swain. *Language Assessment Quarterly, 1*(4), 235–251. https://doi.org/10.1207/s15434311laq0104_3

Freeman, K., & Li, M. (2019). "We are a ghost in the class": First year international students' experiences in the global contact zone. *Journal of International Students, 9*(1), 19–38. https://doi.org/10.32674/jis.v9i1.270

Fuchs, M., Rai, S., & Loiseau, Y. (Eds.). (2019). *Study abroad: Traditions and new directions.* Modern Language Association.

Gallagher, C. E., & Haan, J. E. (2018). University faculty beliefs about emergent multilinguals and linguistically responsive instruction. *TESOL Quarterly, 52*(2), 304–330. https://www.jstor.org/stable/44986993

Gallen, J. (2021). Eportfolios as reflective assessment of social justice. *Irish Journal of Technology Enhanced Learning, 6*(1), 22–28. https://doi.org/10.22554/ijtel.v6i1.89

García, O., Johnson, S. I., & Seltzer, K. (2017). *The translanguaging classroom: Leveraging student bilingualism for learning.* Caslon.

García, O., & Wei, L. (2014a). Language, bilingualism and education. In O. García & L. Wei (Eds.), *Translanguaging: Language, bilingualism and education* (pp. 46–62). Palgrave Macmillan.

García, O., & Wei, L. (Eds.). (2014b). *Translanguaging: Language, bilingualism and education.* Palgrave Macmillan.

Gerwing, T. G., Rash, J. A., Gerwing, A. M. A., Bramble, B., & Landine, J. (2015). Perceptions and incidence of test anxiety. *The Canadian Journal for Scholarship of Teaching and Learning, 6*(3). https://doi.org/10.5206/cjsotl-rcacea.2015.3.3

Gordon, B. L. (2008). Requiring first-year writing classes to visit the writing center: Bad attitudes or positive results? *Teaching English in the Two Year College, 36*(2), 154–163. http://www.ncte.org/journals/tetyc/issues/v36-2

Green, M. F. (2012). Global citizenship: What are we talking about and why does it matter? *Trends and Insights for International Education Leaders, 8*, 1–3.

Green, S. G., Ferrante, C. J., & Heppard, K. A. (2016). Using open-book exams to enhance student learning, performance, and motivation. *Journal of Effective Teaching, 16*(1), 19–35.

Gross-Davis, B. (2009). *Tools for teaching* (2nd ed.). Jossey-Bass.

Guilloteaux, M. J., & Dörnyei, Z. (2008) Motivating language learners: A classroom-oriented investigation of the effects of motivational strategies on student motivation. *TESOL Quarterly, 42*, 55–77. http://dx.doi.org/10.1002/j.1545-7249.2008.tb00207.x

Haan, J., & Gallagher, C. (2022). Situating linguistically responsive instruction in higher education contexts: Foundations for pedagogical, curricular, and institutional support. *TESOL Quarterly, 56*(1), 5–18. https://doi.org/10.1002/tesq.3087

Hall, J. (2013). The impact of rising international student usage of writing centers. *Writing Lab Newsletter, 38*(1–2), 5–9.

Hall, J. K., & Verplaetse, L. S. (Eds.). (2000). *Second and foreign language learning through classroom interaction.* Routledge.

Hammond, Z. (2015). *Culturally responsive teaching and the brain: Promoting authentic engagement and rigor among culturally and linguistically diverse students.* Corwin.

Harris, M. (2017). When responding to student writing, more is better. In C. E. Ball & D. M. Loewe (Eds.), *Bad ideas about writing* (pp. 268–272). Open Access Textbooks, West Virginia University. https://textbooks.lib.wvu.edu/badideas/badideasaboutwriting-book.pdf

Harris, M., & Silva, T. (1993). Tutoring ESL students: Issues and options. *College Composition and Communication, 44*(4), 525–537. https://doi.org/10.2307/358388

Hembree, R. (1988). Correlates, causes, effects, and treatment of test anxiety. *Review of Educational Research, 58*(1), 47–77. https://doi.org/10.3102/00346543058001047

Heng, T. T. (2018). Exploring the complex and non-linear evolution of Chinese international students' experiences in US colleges. *Higher Education Research & Development, 37*(6), 1141–1155.

Hiller, T. B., & Hietapelto, A. B. (2001). Contract grading: Encouraging commitment to the learning process through voice in the evaluation process. *Journal of Management Education, 25*(6), 660–684.

Hirai, R., Frazier, P., & Syed, M. (2015). Psychological and sociocultural adjustment of first-year international students: Trajectories and predictors. *Journal of Counseling Psychology, 62*(3), 438–452. https://doi.org/10.1037/cou0000085

Hofstede, G., Hofstede, G. J., & Minkov, M. (2010). *Cultures and organizations: Software of the mind* (3rd ed.). McGraw-Hill.

hooks, b. (1994). *Teaching to transgress: Education as the practice of freedom.* Routledge.

Horner, B., & Tetreault, L. (Eds.). (2017). *Crossing divides: Exploring translingual writing pedagogies and programs.* University Press of Colorado.

Howard, R. M. (1995). Plagiarisms, authorships, and the academic death penalty. *College English, 57*(7), 788–806. https://doi.org/10.2307/378403

Hsu, C. F., & Huang, I. (2017). Are international students quiet in class? The influence of teacher confirmation on classroom apprehension and willingness to talk in class. *Journal of International Students, 7*(1), 38–52. https://doi.org/10.32674/jis.v7i1.244

Hudley, A. H. C., Mallinson, C., & Bucholtz, M. (2022). *Talking college: Making space for Black language practices in higher education.* Teachers College Press.

Hundley, S. P., & Kahn, S. (2019). *Trends in assessment: Ideas, opportunities, and issues for higher education.* Stylus.

ICEF Monitor. (2019, December 11). *Australian students studying abroad more than ever before.* https://monitor.icef.com/2019/12/australian-students-studying-abroad-more-than-ever-before/

Inoue, A. B. (2019). *Labor-based grading contracts: Building equity and inclusion in the compassionate writing classroom.* University Press of Colorado. https://doi.org/10.37514/per-b.2019.0216.0

Institute of International Education. (n.d.). Open doors fast facts. Retrieved from https://opendoorsdata.org/fast_facts/fast-facts-2021/

Institute of International Education. (2017). *More international students seeking U.S. high school diplomas.* Retrieved from: https://www.iie.org/Why-IIE/Announcements/2017/08/2017-08-09-More-International-Students-Seeking-US-High-School-Diplomas

Institute of International Education. (2020). *Fall 2020 international student enrollment snapshot.* https://www.iie.org/en/Research-and-Insights/Publications/Fall-2020-International-Student-Enrollment-Snapshot

Irons, A., & Elkington, S. (2021). *Enhancing learning through formative assessment and feedback.* Routledge.

Jarvis, S., & Pavlenko, A. (2008). *Crosslinguistic influence in language and cognition.* Routledge.

Jeffries, W. B., & Huggett, K. N. (2014). Teaching large groups. In W. B. Jeffries & K. N. Huggett (Eds.), *An introduction to medical teaching* (2nd ed., pp. 11–26). Springer.

Jenkins, J., & Leung, C. (2019). From mythical "standard" to standard reality: The need for alternatives to standardized English language tests. *Language Teaching, 52*(1), 86–110. https://doi.org/10.1017/S0261444818000307

Jessner, U. (2018). Metacognition in multilingual learning: A DMM perspective. In A. Haukås, C. Bjørke, & M. Dypedahl (Eds.), *Metacognition in language learning and teaching* (pp. 31–47). Routledge. https://doi.org/10.4324/9781351049146-3

Jiang, X. (2012). Effects of discourse structure graphic organizers on EFL reading comprehension. *Reading in a Foreign Language, 24*(1), 84–105. http://hdl.handle.net/10125/66669

Jin, L., & Schneider, J. (2019). Faculty views on international students: A survey study. *Journal of International Students, 9*(1), 84–99. https://doi.org/10.32674/jis.v9i1.268

Khanna, M. M. (2015). Ungraded pop quizzes: Test-enhanced learning without all the anxiety. *Teaching of Psychology, 42*(2), 174–178. https://doi.org/10.1177/0098628315573144

Klenowski, V., Askew, S., & Carnell, E. (2006). Portfolios for learning, assessment and professional development in higher education. *Assessment & Evaluation in Higher Education, 31*(3), 267–286. https://doi.org/10.1080/02602930500352816

Knight, J. (2004). Internationalization remodeled: Definition, approaches, and rationales. *Journal of Studies in International Education, 8*(1), 5–31. https://doi.org/10.1177/1028315303260832

Knoch, U., Rouhshad, A., Oon, S. P., & Storch, N. (2015). What happens to ESL students' writing after three years of study at an English medium university? *Journal of Second Language Writing, 28*, 39–52. https://doi.org/10.1016/j.jslw.2015.02.005

Koka, R. (2017). Formative assessment in higher education: From theory to practice. *European Journal of Social Science Education and Research, 4*(1), 28–34. https://doi.org/10.26417/ejser.v9i1.p28-34

Koo, K. K., Yao, C. W., & Gong, H. J. (2021). "It is not my fault": Exploring experiences and perceptions of racism among international students of color during COVID-19. *Journal of Diversity in Higher Education*. Advance online publication. https://doi.org/10.1037/dhe0000343

Krashen, S. D., Long, M. A., & Scarcella, R. C. (1979). Age, rate and eventual attainment in second language acquisition. *TESOL Quarterly, 13*(4), 573–582. https://doi.org/10.2307/3586451

Kubota, R. (2021). Critical antiracist pedagogy in ELT. *ELT Journal, 75*(3), 237–246. https://doi.org/10.1093/elt/ccab015

Kubota, R., & Lehner, A. (2004). Toward critical contrastive rhetoric. *Journal of Second Language Writing, 13*(1), 7–27. https://doi.org/10.1016/j.jslw.2004.04.003

Kuriyama, S. (2002). The enigma of "time is money." *Japan Review, 14*, 217–230. http://www.jstor.org/stable/25791263

Larson, K. K. (2021). *Labor-based grading contracts in the multilingual FYC classroom: Unpacking the variables* [Doctoral dissertation, University of South Florida]. Digital Commons at University of South Florida. https://digitalcommons.usf.edu/etd/9164/

Leask, B. (2009). Using formal and informal curricula to improve interactions between home and international students. *Journal of Studies in International Education, 13*(2), 205–221. https://doi.org/10.1177/1028315308329786

Lee, E. N., & Orgill, M. (2022). Toward equitable assessment of English language learners in general chemistry: Identifying supportive features in assessment items. *Journal of Chemical Education, 99*(1), 35–48. https://doi.org/10.1021/acs.jchemed.1c00370

Lee, I. (2013). Research into practice: Written corrective feedback. *Language Teaching, 46*(1), 108–119. https://doi.org/10.1017/S0261444812000390

Lee, J. J. (2007). Neo-racism toward international students: A critical need for change. *About Campus, 11*(6), 28–30.

Lee, J. J. (2010). International students' experiences and attitudes at a US host institution: Self- reports and future recommendations. *Journal of Research in International Education, 9*(1), 66–84. https://doi.org/10.1177/1475240909356382

Lee, J. J., & Rice, C. (2007). Welcome to America? International student perceptions of discrimination. *Higher Education, 53*, 381–409. https://doi.org/10.1007/s10734-005-4508-3

Lee, S., & Du, Q. (2021). Quantifying native speakerism in second language (L2) writing: A study of student evaluations of teaching. *Applied Linguistics, 42*(3), 541–568. https://doi.org/10.1093/applin/amaa033

Leki, I. (2001). "A narrow thinking system": Nonnative-English-speaking students in group projects across the curriculum. *TESOL Quarterly, 35*(1), 39–67. https://doi.org/10.2307/3587859

Li, J. (2016). Humility in learning: A Confucian perspective. *Journal of Moral Education, 45*(2), 147–165. https://doi.org/10.1080/03057240.2016.1168736

Li, R. Y., & Kaye, M. (1998). Understanding overseas students' concerns and problems. *Journal of Higher Education Policy and Management, 20*(1), 41–50. https://doi.org/10.1080/1360080980200105

Lillis, T., & Harrington, K. (Eds.). (2015). *Working with academic literacies: Case studies towards transformative practice*. WAC Clearinghouse, Parlor Press. https://wac.colostate.edu/books/perspectives/lillis/

Lin, S.-Y., & Scherz, S. D. (2014). Challenges facing Asian international graduate students in the US: Pedagogical considerations in higher education. *Journal of International Students, 4*(1), 16–33. https://doi.org/10.32674/jis.v4i1.494

Lindahl, K., Tomaš, Z., Krulatz, A., & Farelly, R. (2018). The value of service learning in L2 teacher preparation: Engaging in diverse contexts. In T. Meidl & M. Sulentic Dowell (Eds.), *Service learning initiatives in teacher education programs* (pp. 103–125). IGI Global Publishing.

Lindsey, P., & Crusan, D. (2011). How faculty attitudes and expectations toward student nationality affect writing assessment. *Across the Disciplines, 8*(4). https://wac.colostate.edu/atd/ell/lindsey-crusan.cfm

Lippi-Green, R. (2012). *English with an accent: Language, ideology, and discrimination in the United States*. Routledge.

Littlemore, J., Chen, P. T., Koester, A., & Barnden, J. (2011). Difficulties in metaphor comprehension faced by international students whose first language is not English. *Applied Linguistics, 32*(4), 408–429. https://doi.org/10.1093/applin/amr009

Loewen, S., & Sato, M. (2018). Interaction and instructed second language acquisition. *Language Teaching, 51*(3), 285–329. https://doi.org/10.1017/S0261444818000125

Long, M. H. (1983). Linguistic and conversational adjustments to nonnative speakers. *Studies in Second Language Acquisition, 5*, 177–193. https://doi.org/10.1017/S0272263100004848

Losey, K. M., & Shuck, G. (Eds.). (2021). *Plurilingual pedagogies for multilingual writing classrooms: Engaging the rich communicative repertoires of US students*. Routledge.

Madden-Dent, T. (2021). Advancing equity through culturally responsive social emotional education: Addressing international student integration. In N. Yoder & A. Skoog-Hoffman (Eds.), *Motivating the SEL field forward through equity* (Vol. 21; pp. 159–176). Emerald Publishing. https://doi.org/10.1108/S0749-742320210000021012

Marcucci, P., & Johnstone, D. B. (2007). Tuition fee policies in a comparative perspective: Theoretical and political rationales. *Journal of Higher Education Policy and Management, 29*(1), 25–40. https://doi.org/10.1080/13600800600980015

Matsuda, P. K. (2006). The myth of linguistic homogeneity in U.S. college composition. *College English, 68*(6), 637–651. https://doi.org/10.2307/25472180

Matsuda, P. K., Canagarajah, A. S., Harklau, L., Hyland, K., & Warschauer, M. (2003). Changing currents in second language writing research: A colloquium. *Journal of Second Language Writing, 12*(2), 151–179. https://doi.org/10.1016/S1060-3743(03)00016-X

McLeay, F., & Wesson, D. (2014). Chinese versus UK marketing students' perceptions of peer feedback and peer assessment. *The International Journal of Management Education, 12*(2), 142–150. https://doi.org/10.1016/j.ijme.2014.03.005

Mendelsohn, D. (2002). The lecture buddy project: An experiment in EAP listening comprehension. *TESL Canada Journal, 20*(1), 64–73. https://doi.org/10.18806/tesl.v20i1.939

Mills, J., Wiley, C., & Williams, J. (2019). "This is what learning looks like!": Backward design and the framework in first year writing. *portal: Libraries and the Academy, 19*(1), 155–175. https://doi.org/10.1353/pla.2019.0008

Misra, R., Crist, M., & Burant, C. J. (2003). Relationships among life stress, social support, academic stressors, and reactions to stressors of international students in the United States. *International Journal of Stress Management, 10*(2), 137–157. https://psycnet.apa.org/doi/10.1037/1072-5245.10.2.137

Morales, E. E. (2014). Learning from success: How original research on academic resilience informs what college faculty can do to increase the retention of low socioeconomic status students. *International Journal of Higher Education, 3*(3), 92–102. https://doi.org/10.5430/ijhe.v3n3p92

Morita, N. (2004). Negotiating participation and identity in second language academic communities. *TESOL Quarterly, 38*, 573–603. https://doi.org/10.2307/3588281

Mott-Smith, J., Tomaš, Z., & Kostka, I. (2017). *Teaching effective source use: Classroom approaches that work*. University of Michigan Press.

Nathan, M. J., & Petrosino, A. (2003). Expert blind spot among preservice teachers. *American Educational Research Journal, 40*(4), 905–928. https://doi.org/10.3102/00028312040004905

National Association for College Admissions Counseling. (2013). *Report of the Commission on International Student Recruitment.* https://edit.nacacnet.org/globalassets/documents/publications/international-initiatives/report commissioninternationalstudentrecuitment.pdf

New Zealand Ministry of Education. (2008). *The experiences of international students in New Zealand: Report on the results of the national survey 2007.* http://www.educationcounts.govt.nz/publications/international/22971

Ng, B. (2018). The neuroscience of growth mindset and intrinsic motivation. *Brain Sciences, 8*(2), 20. https://doi.org/10.3390/brainsci8020020

Nilson, L. N. (2016). *Teaching at its best: A research-based resource for college instructors* (4th ed.). Jossey-Bass.

NSW Government. (2012). *Industry action plan: NSW international education and research.* International Education and Research Industry Taskforce. https://www.business.nsw.gov.au/__data/assets/pdf_file/0005/241583/NSW_IER_IAP_final_web_20130208.pdf

O'Dowd, R. (2021). Virtual exchange: Moving forward into the next decade. *Computer Assisted Language Learning, 34*(3), 209–224. https://doi.org/10.1080/09588221.2021.1902201

O'Malley, J. M., & Chamot, A. U. (1990). *Learning strategies in second language acquisition.* Cambridge University Press.

Open Doors. (2022). *International students: All places of origin.* https://opendoorsdata.org/data/international-students/all-places-of-origin/

Oropeza, M. V., Varghese, M. M., & Kanno, Y. (2010). Linguistic minority students in higher education: Using, resisting, and negotiating multiple labels. *Equity & Excellence in Education, 43*(2), 216–231. https://doi.org/10.1080/10665681003666304

Owen, C. (2020, July 27). Best practices for integrating the ADA in the ISS office. NAFSA Blog. https://www.nafsa.org/blog/best-practices-integrating-ada-isss-office

Oxford, R. L. (1999). Anxiety and the language learner: New insights. In J. Arnold (Ed.), *Affect in language learning* (pp. 58–67). Cambridge University Press.

Oxford, R. L. (2017). *Teaching and researching language learning strategies: Self-regulation in context* (2nd ed.). Routledge.

Panadero, E., & Jonsson, A. (2013). The use of scoring rubrics for formative assessment purposes revisited: A review. *Educational Research Review, 9*, 129–144. https://doi.org/10.1016/j.edurev.2013.01.002

Patel, F., & Lynch, H. (2013). Glocalization as an alternative to internationalization in higher education: Embedding positive glocal learning perspectives. *International Journal of Teaching and Learning in Higher Education, 25*(2), 223–230.

Pearson, W. S. (2021). The predictive validity of the Academic IELTS test: A methodological synthesis. *ITL-International Journal of Applied Linguistics, 172*(1), 85–120. https://doi.org/10.1075/itl.19021.pea

Pecorari, D., & Petric, B. (2014). Plagiarism in second-language writing. *Language Teaching, 47*(3), 269–302. https://doi.org/10.1017/S0261444814000056

Pecorari, D., & Shaw, P. (2012). Types of student intertextuality and faculty attitudes. *Journal of Second Language Writing, 21*(2), 149–164. https://doi.org/10.1016/j.jslw.2012.03.006

Phakiti, A., Hirsh, D., & Woodrow, L. (2013). It's not only English: Effects of other individual factors on English language learning and academic learning of ESL international students in Australia. *Journal of Research in International Education, 12*(3), 239–258. https://doi.org/10.1177/1475240913513520

Pica, T., Lincoln-Porter, F., Paninos, D., & Linnell, J. (1996). Language learners' interaction: How does it address the input, output, and feedback needs of L2 learners? *TESOL Quarterly, 30*, 59–84. https://doi.org/10.2307/3587607

Pollock, D. C., & Van Reken, R. E. (2009). *Third culture kids: Growing up among worlds* (Rev. ed.). Nicholas Brealey.

Poyrazli, S., & Lopez, M. D. (2007). An exploratory study of perceived discrimination and homesickness: A comparison of international students and American students. *Journal of Psychology: Interdisciplinary and Applied, 141*(3), 263–280. https://doi.org/10.3200/JRLP.141.3.263-280

Rafoth, B. (2015). *Multilingual writers and writing centers.* University Press of Colorado.

Ramanathan, V., & Atkinson, D. (1999). Individualism, academic writing, and ESL writers. *Journal of Second Language Writing, 8*(1), 45–75. https://doi.org/10.1016/S1060-3743(99)80112-X

Rao, K., & Torres, C. (2017). Supporting academic and affective learning processes for English language learners with universal design for learning. *TESOL Quarterly, 51*(2), 460–472. https://doi.org/10.1002/tesq.342

Rienties, B., Beausaert, S., Grohnert, T., Niemantsverdriet, S., & Kommers, P. (2012). Understanding academic performance of international students: The role of ethnicity, academic and social integration. *Higher Education, 63*(6), 685–700. https://doi.org/10.1007/s10734-011-9468-1

Rifkin, J. (2013). *The European dream: How Europe's vision of the future is quietly eclipsing the American dream.* John Wiley & Sons.

Rocconi, L. M. (2011). The impact of learning communities on first year students' growth and development in college. *Research in Higher Education, 52*(2), 178–193. https://doi.org/10.1007/s11162-010-9190-3

Ross, L. J. (2019, Spring). Speaking up without tearing down. *Learning for Justice.* https://www.learningforjustice.org/magazine/spring-2019/speaking-up-without-tearing-down

Sawir, E. (2013). Internationalisation of higher education curriculum: The contribution of international students. *Globalisation, Societies and Education, 11*(3), 359–378. https://doi.org/10.1080/14767724.2012.750477

Schmidt, R. W. (1990). The role of consciousness in second language learning. *Applied Linguistics, 11*, 129–158. https://doi.org/10.1093/applin/11.2.129

Schreiber, B. R., Lee, E., Johnson, J. T., & Fahim, N. (Eds.). (2021). *Linguistic justice on campus: Pedagogy and advocacy for multilingual students.* Multilingual Matters.

Seal, C. R., Naumann, S. E., Scott, A. N., & Royce-Davis, J. (2010). Social emotional development: A new model of student learning in higher education. *Research in Higher Education Journal, 10*, 1–13.

Seithers, L. C., Amankulova, Z., & Johnstone, C. J. (2022). "Rules you have to know": International and domestic student encounters with institutional habitus through group work. *Journal of International Students, 12*(2), 384–402. https://doi.org/10.32674/jis.v12i2.1651

Selasi, T. (2014). *Don't ask me where I'm from, ask where I'm local* [Video]. TED Conferences. https://www.ted.com/talks/taiye_selasi_don_t_ask_where_i_m_from_ask_where_i_m_a_local?language=en

Shapiro, S. (2012). Citizens vs. aliens: How institutional policies construct linguistic minority students. In Y. Kanno & L. Harklau (Eds.), *Linguistic minority immigrants go to college: Preparation, access, and persistence* (pp. 238–254). Routledge.

Shapiro, S. (2020). Inclusive pedagogy in the academic writing classroom: Cultivating communities of belonging. *Journal of Academic Writing, 10*(1), 154–164. https://doi.org/10.18552/joaw.v10i1.607

Shapiro, S. (2022). *Cultivating critical language awareness in the writing classroom.* Routledge.

Shapiro, S., Cox, M., Shuck, G., & Simnitt, E. (2016). Teaching for agency: From appreciating linguistic diversity to empowering student writers. *Composition Studies, 44*(1), 31–52.

Shapiro, S., & Leopold, L. (2012). A critical role for role-playing pedagogy. *TESL Canada Journal, 29*(2), 121–130. https://doi.org/10.18806/tesl.v29i2.1104

Sherry, M., Thomas, P., & Chui, W. H. (2010). International students: A vulnerable student population. *Higher Education, 60*(1), 33–46. https://doi.org/10.1007/s10734-009-9284-z

Shu, F., Ahmed, S. F., Pickett, M. L., Ayman, R., & McAbee, S. T. (2020). Social support perceptions, network characteristics, and international student adjustment. *International Journal of Intercultural Relations, 74*, 136–148. https://doi.org/10.1016/j.ijintrel.2019.11.002

Silva, T. (1997). On the ethical treatment of ESL writers. *TESOL Quarterly, 31*(2), 359–363. https://doi.org/10.2307/3588052

Singh, N. (2021). The economic contribution of international students in higher education in the United States—A review. *4D International Journal of Management and Science, 12*(1), 6–18.

Smith, M. K., Wood, W. B., Adams, W. K., Wieman, C., Knight, J. K., Guild, N., & Su, T. T. (2009). Why peer discussion improves student performance on in-class concept questions. *Science, 323*(5910), 122–124. https://doi.org/10.1126/science.1165919

Song, B., & August, B. (2002). Using portfolios to assess the writing of ESL students: A powerful alternative? *Journal of Second Language Writing, 11*(1), 49–72. https://doi.org/10.1016/S1060-3743(02)00053-X

Staley, C. (2003). *50 ways to leave your lectern: Active learning strategies to engage first-year students.* Wadsworth/Thomson Learning.

Stoynoff, S. (1997). Factors associated with international students' academic achievement. *Journal of Instructional Psychology, 24*(1), 56–68.

Strayhorn, T. L. (2018). *College students' sense of belonging: A key to educational success for all students* (2nd ed.). Routledge. https://doi.org/10.4324/9781315297293

Styati, E. W., & Irawati, L. (2020). The effect of graphic organizers on ELT students' writing quality. *Indonesian Journal of EFL and Linguistics, 5*(2), 279–293. http://dx.doi.org/10.21462/ijefl.v5i2.283

Sun, X., Hall, G. C. N., DeGarmo, D. S., Chain, J., & Fong, M. C. (2021). A longitudinal investigation of discrimination and mental health in Chinese international students: The role of social connectedness. *Journal of Cross-Cultural Psychology, 52*(1), 61–77. https://doi.org/10.1177/0022022120979625

Swain, M. (1983). Large-scale communicative language testing: A case study. *Language Learning and Communication, 2*, 133–147.

Swain, M. (1985). Communicative competence: Some roles of comprehensible input and comprehensible output in its development. In S. Gass & C. Madden (Eds.), *Input in second language acquisition* (pp. 235–253). Newbury House.

Szafranski, D. D., Barrera, T. L., & Norton, P. J. (2012). Test anxiety inventory: 30 years later. *Anxiety, Stress, and Coping, 25*(6), 667–677. https://doi.org/10.1080/10615806.2012.663490

Tannen, D. (2013). The argument culture: Agonism and the common good. *Daedalus, 142*(2), 177–184. http://www.jstor.org/stable/43297241

Tardy, C. M., & Whittig, E. (2017). On the ethical treatment of EAL writers: An update. *TESOL Quarterly, 51*(4), 920–930. https://doi.org/10.1002/tesq.405

Tavares, V. (2021a). Feeling excluded: International students experience equity, diversity and inclusion. *International Journal of Inclusive Education*, 1–18. https://doi.org/10.1080/13603116.2021.2008536

Tavares, V. (2021b). Multilingual international students at a Canadian university: Portraits of agency. *American Journal of Qualitative Research, 5*(2), 92–117. https://doi.org/10.29333/ajqr/11135

Ting-Toomey, S., & Oetzel, J. G. (2002). Cross-cultural face concerns and conflict styles. In W. B. Gudykunst & B. Mody (Eds.), *Handbook of international and intercultural communication* (2nd ed., pp. 143–164). Sage.

Tomaš, Z., Kostka, I., & Mott-Smith, J. (2020). *Teaching writing* (2nd ed.). TESOL Press.

Tomaš, Z., & Shapiro, S. (2021). From crisis to opportunity: Turning questions about "plagiarism" into conversations about linguistically responsive pedagogy. *TESOL Quarterly, 55*(4), 1102–1113. https://doi.org/10.1002/tesq.3082

Tomaš, Z., VanHorn-Gable, A., and Marniković, S. (2020) TESOL Service-Learning Study Abroad: Examining the Impact on American Pre- and In-Service Teachers and Montenegrin Community Stakeholders. *TEFL-EJ International, 23*, 4. http://www.teslej.org/wordpress/issues/volume23/ej92/ej92a6/

Triandis, H. C. (1993). The contingency model in cross-cultural perspective. In M. M. Chemers & R. Ayman (Eds.), *Leadership theory and research: Perspectives and direction*s (pp. 167–188). Academic Press.

Triandis, H. C. (2001). Individualism-collectivism and personality. *Journal of Personality, 69*, 907–924. https://doi.org/10.1111/1467-6494.696169

Trice, A. G. (2003). Faculty perceptions of graduate international students: The benefits and challenges. *Journal of Studies in International Education, 7*(4), 379–403. https://doi.org/10.1177/1028315303257120

Tummala-Narra, P., & Claudius, M. (2013). A qualitative examination of Muslim graduate international students' experiences in the United States. *International Perspectives in Psychology: Research, Practice, Consultation, 2*(2), 132–147. https://doi.org/10.1037/ipp0000003

U.S. Department of State & U.S. Department of Education. (2021). *Joint statement of principles in support of international education.* https://educationusa.state.gov/sites/default/files/intl_ed_joint_statement.pdf

U.S. News and World Report. (2022). *2022 best global universities ranking.* https://www.usnews.com/education/best-global-universities/rankings

Van Rompay-Bartels, I., & Geessink, J. (2021). Exploring peer feedback on behaviour in the international classroom: A case study on students' experiences and perceptions. *Journal of International Education in Business.* Advance online publication. https://doi.org/10.1108/JIEB-07-2020-0063

Walker, J. (2010). Measuring plagiarism: Researching what students do, not what they say they do. *Studies in Higher Education, 35*(1), 41–59. https://doi.org/10.1080/03075070902912994

Walqui, A. (2006). Scaffolding instruction for English language learners: A conceptual framework. *International Journal of Bilingual Education and Bilingualism, 9*(2), 159–180. https://doi.org/10.1080/13670050608668639

Warner, G., Cohen, R., & Trelles, L. (Hosts). (2021, April 21). How to speak bad English. (No. 7) [Audio podcast episode]. In *Rough Translation.* NPR. https://www.npr.org/2021/04/21/989477444/how-to-speak-bad-english

Wei, M., Heppner, P. P., Mallen, M. J., Ku, T. Y., Liao, K. Y. H., & Wu, T. F. (2007). Acculturative stress, perfectionism, years in the United States, and depression among Chinese international students. *Journal of Counseling Psychology, 54*(4), 385–394. https://doi.org/10.1037/0022-0167.54.4.385

Wei, M., Wang, K. T., & Ku, T. Y. (2012). A development and validation of the Perceived Language Discrimination Scale. *Cultural Diversity & Ethnic Minority Psychology, 18*(4), 340–351. https://psycnet.apa.org/doi/10.1037/a0029453

Weimer, M. (2013). *Learner centered teaching: Five key changes to practice* (4th ed.). Jossey-Bass.

Wick, D., & Willis, T. (2020). International education's potential for advancing social justice. In L. Berger (Ed.), *Social justice and international education* (pp. 11–42). NAFSA.

Wiggins, G. P., & McTighe, J. A. (2005). *Understanding by design.* ASCD.

Williams, H. (2020, November 9–10). *Will students engage if there are no grades? A review of the evidence, and an experiment in ungrading.* 13th Annual International Conference of Education, Research and Innovation, Online Conference. https://doi.org/10.21125/iceri.2020.0605

Wong, L. L. C., & Nunan, D. (2011). The learning styles and strategies of effective language learners. *System, 39*(2), 144–163. https://doi.org/10.1016/j.system.2011.05.004

Yamashita, J. (2002). Mutual compensation between L1 reading ability and L2 language proficiency in L2 reading comprehension. *Journal of Research in Reading, 25*(1), 81–95. https://doi.org/10.1111/1467-9817.00160

Yeager, D. S., & Dweck, C. S. (2020). What can be learned from growth mindset controversies? *American Psychologist, 75*(9), 1269–1284. https://doi.org/10.1037/amp0000794

Yeh, E., Sharma, R., Jaiswal-Oliver, M., & Wan, G. (2022). Culturally responsive social emotional learning for international students: Professional development for higher education. *Journal of International Students, 12*(1), 19–41.

Yu, S., & Lee, I. (2016). Peer feedback in second language writing (2005–2014). *Language Teaching, 49*(4), 461–493. https://doi.org/10.1017/S0261444816000161

Zhang, J., & Goodson, P. (2011). Predictors of international students' psychosocial adjustment to life in the United States: A systematic review. *International Journal of Intercultural Relations, 35*(2), 139–162. https://doi.org/10.1016/j.ijintrel.2010.11.011

Zhang, Y. S. D., & Noels, K. (2021). The frequency and importance of accurate heritage name pronunciation for post-secondary international students in Canada. *Journal of International Students, 11*(3), 608–627. https://doi.org/10.32674/jis.v11i3.2232

Zhang-Wu, Q. (2021). *Languaging myths and realities: Journeys of Chinese international students.* Multilingual Matters.

Appendix A
Classroom Activities

The activities in Table A1 promote interaction in the classroom and increase opportunities for active learning. Many of these activities will also provide you with feedback about student learning and your instructional practices.

Table A1 Classroom activities to promote interaction and active learning

Classroom activities	Description/directions	Possible learning objectives	Tips/ideas for implementation
Icebreaker activities			
Mix and mingle	Provide questions on strips of paper. Give one to each student. Tell students to find a partner with whom to discuss their questions. After each person's question has been addressed, have students exchange papers and find another discussion partner.	• Meet peers and instructor; get to know each other. • Review for test. • Provide peer feedback. • Conduct self-assessment. • Collaborate with peers. • Check comprehension.	**Timing:** Set time limit or goal for the number of questions answered. **Monitoring:** Listen to student exchanges; offer clarification and guidance. **Feedback:** Identify questions that challenge, stir, and motivate; revisit these in class discussion.
Peer interview	Students interview a partner. Next, students introduce their partner to the class, sharing information gleaned from their interviews. (Pairs can exchange introductions with another pair instead of whole-class sharing.)	• Meet peers and instructor; get to know each other. • Discuss and share views on a topic.	**Reducing anxiety:** Introducing a partner rather than oneself can address the need for humility in some cultures and reduce the stress of being on the spot. **Interview topics:** Suggest talking points (e.g., personal information, interest in course, background knowledge of content).
People bingo (See Chapter 2 for a sample bingo board.)	Create two or three unique bingo cards with a statement in each square. Students find others to sign for each statement.	• Meet peers and instructor; get to know each other. • Assess background knowledge. • Review for a test or exam.	**Goals:** Choose content of squares depending on objective (e.g., icebreaker, review, assessment). **Audience:** Consider the most appropriate content for the course level (e.g., graduate, undergraduate). **Promote interaction:** Each peer can only sign once per card, so they have to meet other classmates.
Exploring content			
Muddiest points	Students jot down some points that are unclear to them. They can discuss these with a peer, post them in an online forum, or submit them to the instructor.	• Provide peer feedback. • Provide instructor feedback. • Conduct self-assessment. • Check comprehension.	**Revisiting unclear points:** Consider addressing more complex or critical concepts thoroughly in the subsequent lesson.

Jigsaw reading	Small groups of students receive part or all of a text and a handout with questions about the text. Initial groups complete their section of the handout based on their text. Students regroup so that each new group has one member from each of the original groups. Peers teach one another about their respective texts. By the end of the activity, everyone has a complete "puzzle."	Explore previously unseen text within a class period. Review assigned reading. Practice peer instruction. Collaborate with peers; work as a team.	**Group formation:** Grouping can be a challenge in jigsaw. Label texts so students locate the first group by letter and the second group by number (e.g., A1, A2, A3, B1, B2, B3).
Applying theory to practice			
Case study	Provide students with a situation or extensive real-world problem (e.g., from the news, your professional experience). You might need to provide them with supporting documents. (Excellent STEM field examples can be found at www.nsta.org/case-studies.)	• Connect theory to real-world applications. • Apply analysis, synthesis, and critical-thinking skills.	**Selection:** Make sure the case studies are not overly embedded in culture-specific knowledge; if they are, develop that background knowledge prior to the activities. **Design:** Use real-world scenarios with open-ended problems.
Role-play and simulation	Students assume the role of individuals represented in a real-life context. They prepare using resource materials that the teacher provides (e.g., background of characters, setting, problem or situation). After the role-play, discuss the incidents and alternatives.	• Realize real-life situations in class. • Interact and collaborate with peers. • Analyze an issue from multiple perspectives.	**Example role-play Situations:** historical figures and events, patient and provider in a health clinic, business proposal presentation, investigation of an environmental issue
Poster session	As with professional conferences, students design and present posters in class to showcase final projects or research (individually or in pairs or groups).	• Summarize and synthesize information. • Practice presentation and organization skills. • Conduct oneself professionally.	**Feedback:** Peers can provide feedback and reflections on others' work. **Media:** To avoid the cost and hassle of printing posters, students can create digital posters or presentations.
Panel discussion	Select students to serve as "experts" on a given topic. Each student introduces a topic to the class. The class then asks questions related to the topic. Provide necessary materials for preparation on both sides of the discussion.	• Practice peer instruction. • Invite global and cross-cultural perspectives. • Synthesize, organize, and present information. • Ask and respond to critical questions.	**Learner-centered teaching:** Let the students run the activity. Invite a student to moderate. **Accountability:** Involve "audience" members through a follow-up activity (e.g., 1-minute paper, report on discussion).

Games			
Jeopardy!	Teams choose a category and point value for questions (higher point value corresponds to greater difficulty).	• Review previously learned material (warm-up). • Review for a test or exam.	**Templates:** There are many free Jeopardy! templates available online. PowerPoint has one you can download for free—complete with timers and Daily Doubles!
Who Wants to Be a Millionaire?	Students come to the front of the classroom to be asked multiple-choice questions by a host. As with the TV show, the student can use up to three lifelines (ask a student in the class, search on internet, ask for 50/50 chance).	• Review previously learned material (warm-up). • Review for a test or exam.	**Promote class involvement:** Allow students to serve as host or to generate the questions; ask students to rate the acceptability of the response.
Standing survey	Students move across the room to represent their opinions on various issues; the issues are prepared in advance by the instructor and presented in class as statements. For example, "Stand on the left if you agree with this statement, on the right if you disagree, and in the middle if you are undecided."	• Share and compare views, opinions, and interests. • Discuss difficult (controversial) topics.	**Variation:** This activity is particularly effective as an "energy boost" in long classes, but it can be adapted by giving students "agree" and "disagree" cards that they can hold up.
Password	Students work in pairs or groups, with one student facing the board and the others with their backs to the board. The instructor writes course terms on the board, and the student who can see the word or concept must explain it to the others without using any part of it. Once the student's teammates guess the word, the "explainer" says, "Got it!"	• Review vocabulary. • Conduct self-assessment. • Collaborate with peers. • Practice peer instruction.	**Differentiation:** Students may work at different speeds. The instructor may want to put multiple terms on the board.

Reference

O'Neal, C., Meizlish, D., & Kaplan, M. (2007). *Writing a statement of teaching philosophy for the academic job search* (Occasional Paper). University of Michigan Center for Research on Learning and Teaching, Ann Arbor. http://www.crlt.umich.edu/sites/default/files/resource_files/CRLT_no23.pdf

Appendix B
Rubric Design and Implementation

Building on discussions in Chapters 2 and 4, in this appendix, we provide four sample rubrics (one for a written teaching philosophy statement, one for quantitative work, and two for oral presentations) that illustrate the various options for rubric design (see www.cultofpedagogy.com/holistic-analytic-single-point-rubrics for more information about rubric types). We encourage instructors to experiment with various instruments until they find one that best serves their purposes.

When translating rubric scores into grades, it is important to use ratings that are a fair and accurate reflection of student effort and achievement. Sometimes this means a simple percentage calculation is not the best option. For example, on a rubric that uses a 3-point scoring scale, a score of 2 out of 3 would translate to 67%, which most students would consider a poor grade.

Table B1 *Evaluating a Teaching Philosophy*

Criteria for a "highly effective" rating	Score 4.5–5 = highly effective 4 = moderately effective 3 = ineffective	Comments
Goals for student learning • Goals are clearly articulated and specific, addressing targeted student knowledge, skills, attitudes, and career goals. • Goals are relevant to teaching within the discipline.		
Enactment of goals (teaching method) • The way goals are being targeted is specific. • There are details and rationale about pedagogical approaches. • The approaches are clearly connected to specific goals and are appropriate for those goals. • Specific examples are provided for how the approaches will be used.		
Assessment of goals (measuring student learning) • Specific examples of assessment tools are clearly described. • Assessment tools are aligned with teaching goals and teaching methods. • Assessments reinforce the priorities and context relevant to teaching in the teacher's discipline.		

Inclusive learning environment		
• The statement demonstrates thought for diverse ways of knowing and learning styles. • The statement discusses teacher and learner roles. • The writer demonstrates awareness of current trends in teaching that promote equitable, learner-centered instruction.		
Structure, rhetoric, and language		
• The statement is written clearly and engaging (easy to read). • Jargon is avoided, and teaching terms (e.g., *inductive teaching*) are given specific definitions. • Specific, rich examples are used to strengthen statements of goals, approaches, and assessments. • Grammar and spelling are appropriate for the genre and audience.		
	Total ____ / 25	

Note. Adapted from O'Neal et al., 2007.

Table B2 *Evaluating Quantitative Reasoning Outcomes*

Target performance to meet criteria	Rating scale 5 = target 100% 4 = acceptable 80% 3 = unacceptable 60%	Comments
Build an appropriate model. • The model captures all of the key components of the problem. • The student effectively uses tables, charts, and/or graphs to model the problem.		
Use the model to solve the problem. • The proposed solution is optimal.		
Communicate the results. • The conclusion references tables, charts, graphs, and/or computations. • The writer makes a convincing mathematical argument to justify the conclusion.		
Evaluate the model. • The student identifies the limitations of the model and assumptions that were made in the model.		
	Total ____ / 20	

Note. Adapted from a rubric used by Dr. Stephanie Casey, professor of math education at Eastern Michigan University. Used with permission.

Table B3 *Evaluating Oral Presentations (Separate Ratings for Each Criterion)*

Criteria	Rating	Comments
Relevance of topic (e.g., presentation is related to the course or curriculum unit)	/20	
Use of sources and examples (e.g., presentation includes evidence to support key claims)	/20	

Organization of content (e.g., presentation includes introduction, body, and conclusion)	/20	
Clarity of speech (e.g., presenter uses transition words, clear pronunciation, appropriate rate of speech)	/20	
Preparation and professionalism (e.g., presenter speaks confidently, uses visuals effectively, and stays within the time limit)	/20	
		Total _____ / 100
Other comments or suggestions:		

Note. Adapted from Shawna's courses for first-year students.

Table B4 *Evaluating Oral Presentations (Single Overall Rating)*

Criteria	Rating	Comments
Highly effective • Topic choice is relevant to the course or assignment. • The content is organized (e.g., has a clear introduction, body, conclusion). • Examples are included and the presenter cites sources. • The speech is clear and includes transition words, clear pronunciation, appropriate rate of speech, etc. • The student is prepared and professional (e.g., speaks confidently, uses visuals effectively, and stays within the time limit).	4.5–5	
Moderately effective • Topic choice is only partially relevant. • The content is somewhat organized. • Only limited examples are included, and sources are not cited. • The speech is somewhat clear. • The student is somewhat prepared and professional.	4	
Ineffective • Topic choice is not relevant. • The content is not organized. • There are no examples or sources included. • The speech is not clear. • The student is not prepared or professional.	3	
	Total _____ / 5	
Other comments and suggestions:		

Appendix C
Practice Exercise for Writing Effective Exam Questions

This exercise has been designed to draw your attention to some of the key factors that determine the effectiveness of test and exam questions. First, consider the two versions of the same exam question (from a university math course). How has the instructor improved the original exam question (consider criteria such as clarity, language use, cultural bias, layout, etc.)? Next, think about whether and how you could further modify the exam question.

Original Test Question

Scientists interested in human recall and memory are hypothesizing whether it is easier to memorize words that have "meaning." To address this question, they randomly divided two groups of 15 students from ninth grade, presenting them with two lists of 20 three-letter "words," one containing meaningful words and the other nonsense words. One group was asked to memorize the former and the other group the latter list. The number of words correctly recalled by each student was tabulated, and the resulting data were 12, 15, 12, 12, 10, 3, 7, 11, 9, 14, 9, 10, 9, 5, 13 for meaningful words recalled and 4, 6, 6, 5, 7, 5, 4, 7, 9, 10, 4, 8, 7, 3, 2 for nonsense words recalled. Provide a graph for summarizing and displaying these data sets. On the basis of your graph, what observations can be made regarding how the students assigned the meaningful words performed compared with how the students assigned the nonsense words performed? Summarize what the data and your analysis reveal about the question.

Revised Test Question

Scientists interested in human recall and memory studied this question: "Is it easier to memorize words that have 'meaning'?" To answer the question, they prepared two lists of 20 three-letter "words." One list contained meaningful words (e.g., "cat," "dog"), and the other list contained nonsense words (e.g., "atc," "odg"). They divided a ninth-grade class of 30 students into two random groups of 15 students. Students in one group (G1) memorized the list of meaningful words, and students in the other group (G2) memorized the list of nonsense words. The following table shows the number of words correctly recalled by each student in the two groups:

| G1: *meaningful* | 12 | 15 | 12 | 12 | 10 | 3 | 7 | 11 | 9 | 14 | 9 | 10 | 9 | 5 | 13 |
| G2: *nonsense* | 4 | 6 | 6 | 5 | 7 | 5 | 4 | 7 | 9 | 10 | 4 | 8 | 7 | 3 | 2 |

Task 1

Provide a graph for summarizing and displaying these data sets. Make sure to label and scale your axes!

Task 2

Write a paragraph (at least three sentences) summarizing what the data and your analysis reveal about this question: "Is it easier to memorize words that have meaning?" At a minimum, your summary should compare the centers, shapes, and spreads of the two data sets in context.

These questions have been adapted from ones developed by Dr. Stephanie Casey, professor of math education at Eastern Michigan University. Used with permission.

Appendix D
Grammar Awareness

Building on the discussion of grading in Chapter 4, the following table highlights some of the most common grammatical issues seen in the work of writers for whom English is an additional language. We have included examples of each error and guidance on whether to devote significant attention to that type of error. We hope this table helps instructors answer the following question: Which grammar errors are most likely to interfere with clarity of the writing?

Table D1 Top 10 Most Common Grammatical Issues, Ranked by Impact on Clarity of the Writing

Grammatical issue	Examples	Effect on clarity? What can/should you do?
Verb tense or form (incorrect or shifting)	**Is** she **speak** Japanese? If interest rates **expecting** to fall, stock prices **would have risen**.	This issue can seriously interfere with clarity. Ask students to orally explain what they wish to say. It may also help to ask about "who does what" (agent, verb, object).
Word form	It is **importance** to **investment** time in improving my English grammar.	This issue often interferes with clarity. Offer another word form, telling the student which part of speech is needed (noun, verb, or adjective, in most cases).
Subject-verb agreement	Many investors want to protect their **wealth**, which **are** in banks	This issue often interferes with clarity. It is worth pointing out and asking for clarification.
Plurals (count/ noncount)	This paper includes **many evidences** to support my argument, but I still need to find more **source** in the library.	This issue sometimes interferes with clarity. It is worth pointing out but might not be worth correcting.
Syntax (sentence structure word order)	I asked my instructor what **would be** the due date for the **written second** assignment.	This issue sometimes interferes with clarity. It is worth pointing out and asking for clarification.
General awkwardness or incorrect expressions	I **wish** that we **will** have more time to work on this lab report. On the **third hand** ...	The seriousness of this issue depends on severity. You can start by telling the student whether this is a content issue (i.e., "I don't understand this part") or simply a style issue (i.e., "This just seems strange"). If the latter, you might ignore it. Expect some "written accent."

Nonstandard English or nonacademic register	He **don't** know . . . I'm **gonna** . . .	Address this issue at your discretion; clarity and the need for response depend on the course, genre, student goals, and other factors.
Incorrect punctuation	She said; "I hope to see you, again soon".	This issue can interfere with clarity. When addressing with students, focus on using punctuation to improve readability.
Incorrect or missing article	**The** individuality is [ ] important aspect of American culture.	This issue almost never interferes with clarity. Either correct these directly or ignore them.
Wrong preposition	The essay **from** Foucault is **around** many societal issues.	This issue almost never interferes with clarity. Either correct these directly or ignore them.

Note. Adapted from a chart created by Hidy Basta and Shawna Shapiro in 2007, for use in training workshops for instructors and writing tutors at the University of Washington. Used with permission.

Appendix E
Assigning Participation Points

Most course syllabi include an allocation of some percentage of the overall grade to class participation, yet many instructors do not have a precise plan of action for assigning participation points. Chapter 2 provided one possible approach that relies on evidence of participation. Figure E1 shows sample criteria that you might present to students as acceptable evidence of participation.

Figure E1 Evidence of Participation: Sample Criteria

- ☐ Arrives on time and with necessary materials
- ☐ Contributes during a class discussion
- ☐ Makes comments and contributions that respond to/build on other students' comments
- ☐ Listens attentively during lectures and discussions, as well as during presentations by peers (i.e., is not distracted by technology, is on task)
- ☐ Participates in small-group activities, including peer review
- ☐ Completes in-class assignments (e.g., writing assignments, quizzes, brainstorming sessions)
- ☐ Attends meetings with instructor, peer tutors, teaching assistant, and others as recommended or voluntarily
  May provide evidence of support sought and received through on-campus centers for work in this class
- ☐ Responds to emails from professors and peers and/or engages in online forums as expected for this class
- ☐ Attends departmental film screenings or other special sessions related to this course (if applicable)
- ☐ Contributes effectively as a team member on group projects (if applicable)
- ☐ Additional evidence of active participation in this course
  - •
  - •
  - •

Appendix F
Information About
Student Visas

The following information was adapted from a handout that Karen Edwards, the dean of international student affairs at Grinnell College, uses with her faculty, staff, and administrator colleagues. Her goal in sharing this information is to raise awareness about the many factors impacting students' academic and cocurricular planning based on immigration status.

Although most of the information here is likely to stay the same, visa regulations do change from time to time. Thus, it is important to consult with your institutions' offices (or officers) for international student support, as noted in Chapter 5. Updated information about U.S. visa policies for international students can also be found at https://studyinthestates.dhs.gov. Another useful resource for international offices, faculty, and staff supporting international students is the Association of International Educators, also known as NAFSA (www.nafsa.org).

What Is an F1 Visa?

The most common type of visa for international students is an F-1 Visa—that is, a nonimmigrant visa that allows international students to enter the United States and study at institutions certified by the Student and Exchange Visitor Program (SEVP). Students can only apply for an F-1 visa *after* being accepted to an accredited U.S. institution and being issued the Form I-120. Note that there are other types of visas (e.g., J-1) that some international students, such as short-term exchange students, may hold. It is also important to keep in mind that specific immigration status is confidential.

What Are the Most Important Policies for F-1 Visa Holders?

1. Full-time enrollment is required, with few exceptions.

    a. Students must be enrolled full-time as undergraduate, graduate, or nondegree-seeking students at an accredited institution (e.g., college, university, seminary, language training program) that awards a degree, diploma, or certificate.

b. Students can seek reduced course load authorization in three scenarios: first-semester language difficulties, a documented medical condition, or the final semester before graduation.

c. Only one online or distance education class or three credits per academic term may count toward the "full course load" requirement.

3. International students can typically participate in off-campus study opportunities, but there are visa issues to consider, and advanced planning is essential.

4. F-1 students who are considering a personal, medical, or military leave or a mid-program transfer to another U.S. school should consult the institution's office for international student support. Approval is required, and students cannot typically stay in the United States during a leave.

5. Enrolling in a summer class at another U.S. school may be allowed, but campus employment could be limited to the student's primary institution.

6. On-campus employment is limited to 20 hours per week while school is in session. Students may be able to work more hours during breaks. Off-campus employment options vary from institution to institution, so check with the institution's office of international student support. On-campus employment eligibility ends with graduation so alumni who pursue post-baccalaureate positions must secure authorization (typically via Optional Practical Training [OPT]; learn more at www.uscis.gov/working-in-the-united-states/students-and-exchange-visitors/optional-practical-training-opt-for-f-1-students).

7. Choosing a "major" introduces additional nuances for F-1 students because it may limit their access to U.S. work opportunities. Practical training benefits are only applicable when work is directly related to the declared major. In addition, make note of the following:

a. All majors have access to 12 months of employment authorization via OPT.

b. STEM majors may be eligible for up to 24 additional months of authorization via STEM OPT (see the list of programs at www.ice.gov/doclib/sevis/pdf/stemList2022.pdf).

c. Education licensure is available to F-1 students. U.S. licensure is recognized in some other countries, but there are unique considerations. Interested students should consult with the office for international student support.

d. International students who are interested in attending U.S. medical schools should consult early on with international student offices and health professions staff at their institution, as acceptance rates are extremely competitive, and most U.S. medical schools are closed to noncitizens.

7. Students wishing to engage in unpaid or volunteer endeavors should also consult their institution's office for international student support.

8. Before an enrolled F-1 student may work off campus (broadly defined, for paid or unpaid experiences), they may need to secure Curricular

Practical Training (CPT) authorization. The institution's office for international student support may be able to authorize CPT for eligible students who secure an internship. Eligibility for CPT requires at least two consecutive semesters in F-1 status, and the work must be directly related to the student's declared major. CPT is required if and when the student is inside the United States, regardless of the employer location.

9. The office for international student support should provide assistance to F-1 seniors and alumni who pursue postgraduation options in the United States.

    a. Seniors who will proceed to graduate studies in the United States must request a Student and Exchange Visitor Information System (SEVIS) Release.

    b. Seniors who will pursue U.S.-based work in their major must apply for 12 months of Post-Completion OPT. (It is recommended that students begin the application process as soon as the regulations allow, as processing times can vary.)

    c. Eligible alumni who wish to apply for 24 additional months of STEM OPT also work with the office for international student support throughout the full authorization period.

10. F-1 students who graduate early must shorten their F-1 program via the office for international student support.

    NOTE: F-1 students who will <u>not</u> graduate on time must process a program extension *prior to* the I-20 end date. It is possible that a program extension requires funding documentation, and it may jeopardize Post-Completion OPT. A program cannot be extended for online courses.

Appendix G
English Proficiency Tests and Admissions Policies

Most U.S. institutions of higher education require a minimum proficiency level in English for admission to academic programs. Institutions have the freedom to establish their specific language requirements in terms of the minimum scores accepted for undergraduate and graduate admissions. (See Table G1 for the range of requirements at our respective institutions.)

Generally, the commonly accepted tests of English proficiency at U.S. universities and colleges include the Test of English as a Foreign Language (TOEFL), the International English Language Testing System exam (IELTS), and the Cambridge Assessment English (CAE), and (more recently) the Duolingo English Test (DET). For the most part, prospective students must access the exams at certified testing centers in their home countries prior to submitting their applications. Some institutions require additional tests administered on site upon a student's arrival, which may be used to place the student into particular courses or to inform the student's self-placement decisions.

Although the goal of English language proficiency tests is to ensure that students are prepared for the academic and linguistic demands of the curriculum, some experts have raised concerns about how decisions are made around these tests. Questions we need to be asking at our institutions include the following:

- Who makes decisions about how English language test scores are used at my institution?

- Which tests do my institution and program accept?

- What minimum scores are required for admissions or placement into particular programs or courses?

It is also important to keep in mind that even if a student meets the test score requirement, they may still need support to succeed academically. Simply raising required test scores is not an effective way to foster success for international students. Thus, in addition to being informed about testing policies, we should stay engaged in institution-wide conversations about academic and linguistic support for all students, regardless of their test scores. (See Chapter 5 for more on this topic.)

Table G1 English Language Proficiency for Admission to Our Universities

We compiled the following information related to English language proficiency tests and scores from the admissions webpages at our universities to show how much policies can vary across institutions.

Middlebury College	Eastern Michigan University	University of Colorado Boulder
Middlebury has no minimum score that would automatically eliminate an application. The average TOEFL score for matriculated students is 109. For IELTS, successful candidates typically receive a score of 7.5 or higher.	• TOEFL: 61 iBT (TOEFL Home Edition also accepted) • IELTS: 6.0 (IELTS Indicator also accepted) • Michigan English Test (MET): 48 • Pearson English Language Test (PTE): 44 • Duolingo: 95 (Students admitted based on Duolingo English Test scores will be required to take an English proficiency exam upon arrival and may be placed into English as an additional language courses, depending on their performance on this exam.)	**Engineering** • TOEFL: 83 • IELTS: 6.5 • Duolingo: 105 **All other majors** • TOEFL: 75 • IELTS: 6.5 • Duolingo: 100

Appendix H
Professional Journals
for Further Reading

In this appendix, we offer some of the professional and scholarly journals that focus on support for international students and students for whom English is an additional language. We hope this list serves as a starting place for readers who would like to further their knowledge in applied linguistics and related fields.

For more recommended reading and resources, check out the links at our companion website to this volume (www.tesol.org/FISS).

English for Specific Purposes

(journals.elsevier.com/english-for-specific-purposes)

This journal focuses on disseminating research related to the teaching and learning of English for use in specific contexts or communities, such as business, health, and science. The journal explores many topics, including material design, testing techniques, language teaching approaches, and curriculum design.

Journal of English for Academic Purposes

(journals.elsevier.com/journal-of-english-for-academic-purposes)

This journal targets teachers, learners, and researchers engaged in all aspects of the study and use of English in academic contexts. Among the many topics it addresses are institutional policies, intercultural communication, international student experiences, and internationalization.

Journal of International Students

(jistudents.org)

This journal publishes articles on a wide range of topics, including cross-cultural studies (e.g., culture shock, acculturation, self-esteem), intercultural communication, internationalization, expectations of international teaching assistants, and English language proficiency.

Journal of Research in International Education

(jri.sagepub.com)

This journal focuses on the significance and implications of "education for international understanding." It explores many topics, including international student identity, internationalization, curriculum design, and culture shock.

Journal of Second Language Writing

(journals.elsevier.com/journal-of-second-language-writing)

This journal is committed to publishing research and discussions that explore second and foreign language writing and writing instruction. Articles address various topics, including multilingual writers' writing processes, responding to multilingual writers' texts, multilingual writing instruction, and multilingual writers' attitudes.

Journal of Studies in International Education

(jsi.sagepub.com)

This journal includes articles related to various aspects of the internationalization of higher education. Topics include internationalization policies, internationalization curriculum development, and challenges faced by international students. Target audiences include higher education administrators, faculty, researchers, and policymakers.

TESOL Quarterly

(tesol.org/tq)

This journal compiles research and discussions on English language teaching and learning. Teachers of English to speakers of other languages (TESOL) share their research findings and continually grow the knowledge base for teaching and learning English as an additional language. The target audience includes teachers of English as an additional language, researchers, and applied linguists.

TESOL Journal

(tesol.org/tj)

This journal showcases practitioner-oriented articles based on current theory and research in the field of teaching English to speakers of other languages. The journal is a forum for exploring the ways that research and theory can inform, shape, and ground teaching practices and perspectives.

This book is a copublication of **TESOL International Association** and NAFSA: Association of International Educators.

**tesolpress**

TESOL International Association advances professional expertise in English language teaching to speakers of other languages in multilingual contexts worldwide through professional learning, research, standards, and advocacy.

TESOL Press, the publishing division of TESOL International Association, supports excellence in the field of English language teaching through a full range of publications. TESOL authors are leading experts in the field and include experienced researchers, classroom teachers, and students.

www.tesol.org

To order this and other TESOL Press publications: **bookstore.tesol.org**

NAFSA
Connecting People. Changing the World.™

NAFSA: Association of International Educators is the world's largest nonprofit association dedicated to international education and exchange. NAFSA serves the needs of more than 10,000 members and international educators worldwide at more than 3,500 institutions, in more than 160 countries. NAFSA believes that international education advances learning and scholarship, fosters understanding and respect among people of diverse backgrounds and perspectives, is essential for developing globally competent individuals, and builds leadership for the global community.

www.nafsa.org

To order this and other NAFSA publications: shop.nafsa.org